BRIGHT NOTES

WALDEN TWO
BY
B.F. SKINNER

Intelligent Education

Nashville, Tennessee

BRIGHT NOTES: Walden Two
www.BrightNotes.com

No part of this publication may be used or reproduced in any manner whatsoever without written permission, except in the case of brief quotations in critical articles and reviews. For permissions, contact Influence Publishers http://www.influencepublishers.com.

ISBN: 978-1-645420-38-5 (Paperback)
ISBN: 978-1-645420-39-2 (eBook)

Published in accordance with the U.S. Copyright Office Orphan Works and Mass Digitization report of the register of copyrights, June 2015.

Originally published by Monarch Press.
Peter Ruppert, 1976
2020 Edition published by Influence Publishers.

Interior design by Lapiz Digital Services. Cover Design by Thinkpen Designs.

Printed in the United States of America.

Library of Congress Cataloging-in-Publication Data forthcoming.
Names: Intelligent Education
Title: BRIGHT NOTES: Walden Two
Subject: STU004000 STUDY AIDS / Book Notes

CONTENTS

1) Introduction to B. F. Skinner   1

2) "Walden Two" and the Utopian Tradition   22

3) Strategies, Themes, Issues - Part 1   31

4) Strategies, Themes, Issues - Part 2   48

5) Characterization in "Walden Two"   62

6) Bibliography   79

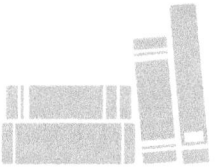

INTRODUCTION TO B. F. SKINNER

B. F. Skinner intended his utopian novel, *Walden Two* (1948), to be read as a serious and positive image of "the good life." Immediately upon publication, the work was alternately praised and condemned by critics. Many readers felt that Skinner's *Walden Two* community was indistinguishable from such famous anti-utopian patterns as Orwell's *1984* and Huxley's *Brave New World*. Life magazine called it "a travesty of the good life," and Joseph Wood Krutch in his book *The Measure of Man* (1954) attacked Skinner's novel vigorously as an "ignoble utopia which describes the contented life led by inmates of an institution." Others admired *Walden Two* as an imaginative discourse on the possibilities of social organization. In fact, in 1967, a group of dedicated young communalists set up a community based on the principles of Skinner's novel. This community, Twin Oaks, still exists today and we shall later consider some of the difficulties and successes that this community has experienced.

Today *Walden Two* continues to arouse sharp, passionate and often divisive reaction. It is seemingly impossible to remain neutral toward the image of life inside Skinner's behaviorally engineered society. On the one hand, Skinner projects a vision of what life could be inside utopia: happy, secure, productive, creative; on the other hand, this vision has come to be feared as a nightmare depicting a potential dictatorship in which human beings are completely conditioned,, controlled, and reduced to automatons without even a conscious life.

WHY SUCH PASSIONATE REACTIONS?

What is it about *Walden Two* that has aroused such division and hostility? What is it about ourselves that Skinner is challenging, or perhaps revealing? And why does this image of "the good life" produce such anxiety and fear in many critics?

Skinner remains puzzled by the negative reactions to his blueprint for utopia. In his view, *Walden Two* is simply a proposal for a more rational world. In applying the findings of his scientific analysis of behavior to the problems of communal living, Skinner thinks he is providing us with the real possibility of a world which is peaceful, constructive, and efficient. *Walden Two,* after all, depicts a society which provides the basic necessities of life without violence, aggression, or exploitation. It is a community in which the arts, sciences, and education flourish, in which everyone performs rewarding work, and in which the members are cooperative, content, and live in a pleasant environment.

What is it about *Walden Two,* then, that has aroused such hostile criticism? Is *Walden Two* a proposal for totalitarian thinking? What fundamental human values is Skinner questioning? We will address ourselves to these and other questions surrounding the controversy over Skinner's views. Since there seems to be a great deal of misunderstanding about the implications of Skinner's novel on both sides of the argument, we will try to maintain an objective, critical perspective. We will point out where Skinner's critics may be have overreacted in the past, but we will also stress shortcomings and weaknesses that we detect in Skinner's premises.

PROFESSOR BURRHUS FREDERICK SKINNER

is probably the most influential contemporary academic psychologist. His contributions to the field of behavioral science include such basic textbooks as *Science and Behavior* (1953), *Verbal Behavior* (1957), and many others. His own unique psychology of "operant behaviorism" has made him in the eyes of many people the most prominent figure in contemporary Behaviorism. Skinner's brand of behavioral psychology has evolved from the early days of John B. Watson, generally considered the founder of Behaviorism, who in 1913 published the manifesto for the movement, *Psychology as the Behaviorist Views It*. Since then Behaviorism has become the dominant school of American Psychology. Although Skinner acknowledges the influence of Watson on his own views, he has also expressed criticism of this early period. Skinner feels that these early behaviorists expended too much time and effort in repudiating the introspective study of man and made extreme claims for their own science.

Contemporary behaviorism (neo-behaviorism) is represented by many prominent behaviorists, and there is some diversity in the movement. Skinner is perhaps the most influential and the most radical. He believes unequivocally in the importance and beneficence of his science. Traditional views of man, he argues, have been around for centuries, but they have not helped us much and are mainly responsible for the problems we face today. Skinner is convinced that Behaviorism offers an effective alternative to the mistakes of the past.

To most laymen, however, Skinner is known primarily for the famous Skinner box (a device that allows the experimenter in the laboratory to control the environment of pigeons or rats) and for the equally famous Aircrib or "baby box," which plays a role in the *Walden Two* nurseries. Furthermore, Skinner has achieved considerable fame in the design of programmed instruction on teaching machines.

SKINNER'S LITERARY INTERESTS

Although Skinner's prominence in the field of psychology rests on his development of methods and techniques used in the scientific study of behavior, he has also maintained a continued interest in literature. In high school, he played the piano and wrote poetry, and as an undergraduate he majored in English literature. After receiving encouragement from Robert Frost, Skinner decided on a career as a writer. Unfinished novels and other setbacks induced him to pursue his interests in human and animal behavior.

He plunged into his graduate studies at Harvard University, maintaining rigorous schedules for study and research. After completing his Ph.D. degree (1931), he spent five years in the laboratory doing research under a National Research Fellowship and as a Junior Fellow in the Harvard Society of Fellows. Subsequently, Skinner held teaching positions at the University of Minnesota (1936-1945) and at Indiana University, where he was chairman of the Psychology Department (1945-1948). In 1948, he returned to Harvard University, where he is now Edgar Pierce Professor of Psychology.

GENESIS OF "WALDEN TWO"

In his autobiographical sketch, Skinner relates that he never really gave up his interest in literature. After his conversion to science, he began to look at literature as a field for analysis and began work on his book *Verbal Behavior* on which he labored for twenty-three years. His interest in literature was further reinforced by his marriage in 1936 to Yvonne Blue, who was also a major in English. Subsequently, Skinner taught courses in the psychology of literature. The general idea for *Walden Two*, Skinner explains, came out of a dinner-party discussion with a friend in 1945. The discussion centered on young men returning from World War II and the kind of society they were returning to. Although he did not take the idea seriously at first, he began to think about the possibilities of applying the experimental attitude to communal living. Soon he found himself completely wrapped up in the project. Usually a slow, painstaking writer, Skinner relates that *Walden Two* turned into an inspirational experience. He finished the novel in seven weeks. He further describes the experience as a "venture in self-therapy" in which he was trying to reconcile two sides of his own personality as reflected in the fictional Burris and Frazier.

The high point of Skinner's research career came after *Walden Two* and after his return to Harvard. In collaboration with Charles B. Ferster he published *Schedules of Reinforcement* in 1957. Practical applications of their findings led to Skinner's work with psychotic patients and retardates, a field in which many of Skinner's findings are still being applied.

ENDS VERSUS MEANS

Throughout his writings, Skinner has expressed and continues to express an abiding faith in his science of man. He claims that it provides him with an "effective experimental approach" to the study of human behavior, and he remains convinced that his position will ultimately triumph. Skinner's views on the control of behavior and his strong stand on the question of freedom vs. determinism (especially in *Beyond Freedom and Dignity*, 1971) challenge some of our most cherished beliefs and have aroused passionate attack. Although he has been variously attacked as a Machiavellian, a Communist, and a Fascist, Skinner claims that he favors the ends of a democratic philosophy, although not the means. This is actually the crux of Skinner's position. He is dismayed at the fact that human behavior continues to be shaped by a system of aversive control (punitive methods), and he feels that if man is to have a future he must replace the present system of negative reinforcement with a technology of positive reinforcement. This is the only hope Skinner sees if we are to maintain our democratic institutions and develop our capabilities. By eliminating aversive control, he believes, we can extend the potentials of an experimental analysis of behavior into a scientific and beneficent program of control. Since man is moved by forces outside himself, Skinner argues, man is controlled anyway, but why leave these forces up to chance? Why not control and manipulate them for man's benefit? Only in this way, Skinner believes, can we arrive at a new humanism.

BASIC PREMISES OF SKINNERIAN PSYCHOLOGY

In order to understand fully the implications of Skinner's novel, *Walden Two*, it is very helpful to consider in some detail the basic premises on which Skinner's "science of human behavior" is based. This will help clarify many of the **episodes** in the book, and, more importantly, will sketch out the principle of "operant conditioning" on which Skinner's utopia is founded. A full consideration of Skinner's psychology is, of course, beyond the scope of this study. The reader who is interested in further reading on the technical aspects should consult the bibliographies at the conclusion of this monograph. We will consider here only those aspects of Skinner's psychology that will enhance our understanding of the novel.

STRATEGY OF BEHAVIORISM

In general, Skinner feels that psychology has suffered in the past because it has attempted to explain human behavior in terms of feelings, attitudes, and states of mind. Accordingly, Skinner thinks that psychology has wasted a lot of time in constructing theories about mind, personality, subjective concepts of the self, and subjective attitudes of the individual. Skinner suggests a more practical approach: psychology should concern itself only with behavior that is observable in the world in which it occurs. What goes on inside the body and skull, Skinner feels, is the domain of the physiologist and biochemist. Introspection, as a means of finding out what goes on inside a person, has been vastly overrated, in Skinner's view, and is not a scientifically reliable way to study behavior. Instead, Skinner's "science of behaviorism" sees the individual as an organism that lives and behaves in an environment, and it is the interaction between the organism and the environment that is of interest in Skinner's psychology. Skinner has repeatedly stated that human behavior is a product of genetic endowment and environmental influence. The emphasis falls on environmental influence since this aspect is more accessible for observation. Physiology and biochemistry have not yet thoroughly analyzed the processes inside the body, but the role that environment plays in shaping human behavior, Skinner argues, can easily be studied by manipulating the environment and observing the effects on behavior. The aim of Skinner's behaviorism is twofold: to describe and explain human behavior, and to change and predict behavior.

We can already see that Skinner's way of doing psychology involves sweeping changes in our traditional image of man and in some of our most cherished ideas about ourselves. Skinner raises many questions about ethics, culture, religion, and human nature itself. Many people are disturbed by his formulations.

Skinner defines his kind of neo-behaviorism as the philosophy of the science of behavior. The questions it asks are: 1) Why do people behave as they do?, and 2) How can a person be brought to behave in a certain way? In trying to answer these questions, Skinner insists that mentalistic explanations (feelings, states of mind) must be by-passed. Only objectively observed facts should be considered, and they should be considered only in relation to the individual's prior environmental history. It is important to note that Skinner does not say that the "inner life" or "mind" should be entirely disregarded. He simply says that these inner states cannot be described accurately, reliably, scientifically. Hence they cannot be scientifically ascertained. Since we ourselves often do not know why we behave as we do and since this private world is not ascertainable, Skinner's objection is that the methods of introspection in trying to reveal this "world within the skin" have actually obfuscated the facts and impeded the development of psychology.

OPERANT BEHAVIOR

Skinner class his form of behaviorism "operant behaviorism." It is important to pinpoint precisely what Skinner means by operant behavior since there seems to be a great deal of misunderstanding of this concept. One should begin by making a distinction between operant behavior and reflex behavior. Reflex behavior is best evidenced in Pavlov's famous experiment with salivating dogs. Pavlov's principle was simple enough: the stimulus (food) produces a reaction (salivating) in a hungry dog. By simultaneously ringing a bell with the introduction of the stimulus, the experimenter soon conditions the dog to associate the sound of the bell with food, and the dog will begin to salivate when he hears the bell even if there is no food present. Hence, reflex behavior is essentially involuntary behavior. Skinner stresses that operant behavior is voluntary; that is, it is behavior that is "felt" to be "under the control" of the behaving organism. Furthermore, in Skinner's operant psychology, the organism "operates" on its environment (by pulling levers, pecking at discs, etc.), as opposed to the passive conditioning of Pavlov's experiment. It is also important to note that operant behavior is voluntary but not uncaused, i.e., it is not inner-motivated or the result of free will. We shall see later that operant conditioning is the central concept on which *Walden Two* is built.

The basic notion behind Skinner's operant behavior is that all organisms, including man, are to a large extent shaped by the consequences of their behavior. Operant behaviorism seeks to study the consequences that actions have had on the organism in the past. There are many things in the environment that are rewarding: food, water sexual contact, etc. These rewards tend to sustain a given behavior which is thus more likely to recur. For Skinner, behavior is strengthened by its consequences. These consequences are called "reinforcers." For example, behavior that results in obtaining food is "reinforced" by the consequence of obtaining food and is therefore likely to recur. Skinner has studied the effects of various kinds of "reinforcers" (rewards) on behavior.

POSITIVE REINFORCEMENT

Positive reinforcement strengthens and maintains the kind of behavior that produces the reinforcement. For example, my cat, Maxwell, rings a bell suspended from the inside door knob whenever he wants to go out. His behavior (ringing the bell) is reinforced by my opening the door. (There are times when I wonder who is conditioning whom!) In Skinner's view, behavior that recurs frequently must have been rewarded in this way.

NEGATIVE REINFORCEMENT

Skinner defines negative reinforcement as that which strengthens and maintains the kind of behavior that reduces or removes the stimulus. For example, my other cat, Morris, tries to remove his flea collar because it irritates his sensitive skin. Negative reinforcement, then, is behavior which brings escape from an aversive (in this case, irritating) condition.

PUNISHMENT

Punishment is sometimes confused with negative reinforcement, but in Skinner's language it refers to a stimulus that removes behavior from an organism's repertoire. It is essentially the opposite of reinforcing. For example, if I substituted an electric shock each time my cat Max rings the bell, he would remove that behavior from his repertoire and do something else whenever he wants to go out. We shall see later that Skinner thinks of punishment as an ineffective and shabby way to control behavior because it has negative side-effects - anxiety, suppressed behavior, deviant behavior.

AVERSIVE CONTROL

By aversive control, Skinner means any kind of control that is maintained through aversive stimuli: threats, coercion, deprivation, fear, etc. Skinner feels that our educational system relies heavily on this kind of control to its own detriment. In *Walden Two*, this kind of control has been eliminated.

SCHEDULES OF REINFORCEMENT

Skinner has studied the effects of various kinds of schedules of reinforcement on the behavior of the organism. These schedules refer essentially to the patterns of dispensing rewards. Some of the results seem obvious, but there have been some unexpected or at least revealing results. For example, Skinner has shown that consistent reinforcement (a reward each time a response is emitted) leads to a low tolerance for frustration and a lack of perseverance. Intermittent reinforcement, when reward does not occur every time, but rather occurs unevenly or irregularly, tends to bring about greater response strength and an increase in frustration tolerance. There are a variety of such schedules which we cannot go into here. Most important are the fixed ratio schedule and the variable ratio schedule. In the fixed ratio schedule, reward is dispensed for a fixed number of responses. This kind of schedule has been found to increase the persistence of a particular response and to make the organism more industrious. It is the kind of reinforcement one would find in industries that use the piece-work system. The variable ratio schedule dispenses rewards on an irregular or random basis. Such a schedule produces great perseverance. This may explain why the slot-machine has such a powerful effect over some people.

CONTINGENCIES OF REINFORCEMENT

The term "contingencies of reinforcement" refers to an important notion in Skinner's psychology. We have seen that for

Skinner all behavior is determined directly or indirectly by its consequences. Contingencies of reinforcement are important because for Skinner they explain how, in a given environment, behavior has certain kinds of consequences. The term refers to the subtle interdependence between the environment and the individual, to the relationship between the situation in which the behavior occurs and its consequences. Skinner distinguishes "contingency shaped" behavior from "rule governed behavior," giving as an example the difference between learning a language on the basis of memorizing its grammar (rules) and learning the language by the day-to-day process of conversing in it with native speakers (contingency shaped behavior). Thus, contingency shaped behavior is behavior learned through a lived experience, whereas rule governed behavior is behavior learned on the basis of following rules. "Contingencies of reinforcement," then, are the combined forces of the total environment in which the behavior is learned.

BEHAVIORIST VIEW OF MAN

Skinner's "behavioral analysis" of man rests on the assumption that the individual is an organism with inherited physiological characteristics and a "repertoire of behavior" created by the contingencies of reinforcement to which he is exposed during his lifetime. As an individual, he is the result of many genetic and environmental conditions, and as such he is unique. No one else has the same genetic endowment (unless a twin) or the same personal history. But his uniqueness is the product of these sources. This distinguishes Skinner's view from what he calls "mentalistic views" in which a person's behavior is shaped by inner qualities like sensations, imagination, intelligence, dreams, moods, intentions, free choice, etc. Skinner's view of man assumes determinism. For Skinner, man is not an originating, free, creative agent. Skinner admits that he cannot prove decisively that human behavior is completely determined, but, like Frazier, he must assume it if his science of behavior is to have a foundation. Skinner believes that as we learn more and more about man, complete determinism will be demonstrated. It is important to note that Skinner does grant man the capability of manipulating the variables in his own environment which in turn control his behavior, but we must immediately add that this desire to control the variables does not originate in the mind as free choice, but rather is determined by the contingencies in the environment. Determinism is the key assumption in Skinner's view of man.

PROBLEM OF CONTROL

The question that has aroused the most virulent resistance to Skinner's propositions is the question of control. For Skinner, a person's behavior is controlled by his genetic and environmental "history" rather than by the person himself, and it is simply a fact for Skinner that human behavior is always controlled. Control is as much a part of life as breathing and reproduction. There is simply no way of life that can do without control. Governments, religions, educational systems, Skinner tells us, all exert control, but this control is often covert or camouflaged. Teachers, therapists and priests will try to make the person think that he is controlling his own behavior when in fact they are controlling and managing his behavior.

What Skinner objects to is the fact that control is usually exerted in aversive ways (use of threat, coercion, punishment) or to exploit others. People oppose controls, Skinner argues, because most of the controlling practices in our culture have been based on aversive means. In the family the child is controlled by punishment or fear of punishment; our teaching techniques are blatantly aversive (we place the student in a threatening environment from which he can escape only by learning); our government controls us through punitive measures. What is required, Skinner argues, is not less control but better control. Better control, Skinner asserts, could be exerted if society adopted a generous and consistent dose of positive reinforcement. This would lead to better ways of teaching, better and more pleasant working conditions, better systems of government, and even more leisure time for art, music and literature.

The all-important question, however, becomes: Who is to design and maintain control? Skinner's reply is that no one person will control because no one can be outside the reinforcement process. Mankind in general will produce environments in which people will behave more and more "successfully." The social environment in which a person lives will generate rules, laws, patterns of behavior which will fluctuate and evolve with time. Skinner sees the evolution of culture as a reciprocal process between man and his environment. But the evolution of culture has in the past been subject to chance mutations, as in natural selection in biology. Skinner sees no virtue in leaving things up to chance. Leaving things up to chance in the past is reflected in our current problems: inconsistent, paradoxical, conflicting behavior, and despair. This is due to inconsistent and poor reinforcement. The science of human behavior, Skinner argues, is capable of manipulating and designing the contingencies of reinforcement in a way that natural selection cannot. Things can go wrong in the process of chance evolution, but they can be rectified by explicit design. Skinner's answer as to who is to re-design the contingencies of reinforcement remains vague. His critics are not satisfied with his answer. Somebody has to decide what the contingencies of reinforcement are going to be, they argue, and groups are unlikely to agree on such important decisions.

GENERAL CRITICISM OF SKINNER'S PSYCHOLOGY

Skinner's psychology, operant behaviorism, is one of many diverse psychologies struggling for dominance. It differs from others in its premises, approaches, and methods. Many of these other schools of psychology have leveled serious criticism against Skinner. We will consider here only the most frequent and potentially most damaging criticism of Skinner. Since *Walden Two* is based on the principles of operant behaviorism, many of these criticisms apply to *Walden Two* as well.

Does Skinner Ignore Human Complexity?

One frequent criticism of Skinner's psychology is that it does not recognize the complexity of human beings. Skinner's psychology is psychology without a "psyche" because he neglects what goes on inside the human being, neglects consciousness, feelings, mind. Skinner's critics insist that there is a great deal that goes on inside a person which never appears as observable behavior. In attempting to make his analysis of human behavior scientific (a curious 19th Century kind of science, his critics assert), Skinner has diminished and oversimplified human behavior. Skinner has outraged many people by insisting that such cherished concepts as human freedom and dignity, the human capacity for choice, and the responsibility for individual choice are mere historical fictions. In *Beyond Freedom and Dignity* (1971), Skinner argues that freedom and dignity are outdated relics of former mystical beliefs that should be discarded. Skinner's critics feel that he offers us a simple image of man and his world, perhaps an oversimplified image of man and a less than human world. This is a serious criticism that should not be taken lightly. We will take up this issue when we discuss the image of man in *Walden Two*.

Does Skinner Reduce Man to an S-R Mechanism?

Another criticism, similar to the first-one, is that Skinner reduces man to a simple stimulus-response mechanism. This would make the human being scarcely more than a puppet, machine, or robot. Skinner does not say, however, that operant behaviorism can predict precisely what people will do, but rather that genetic and environmental conditions determine the probability of a response. For example, the likelihood of my going to the movies is dependent on all kinds on contingencies: free time, transportation, the subject matter of the film, the director, the actors, people I'm likely to meet there, etc. This is certainly different from the stimulus-response image of man that is sometimes attributed to Skinner.

Does Skinner Discount Originality and Creativity?

Another frequent objection is that Skinner's psychology is restrictive in the sense that it cannot account for art, language, science, music, literature, etc.; in other words, it leaves no room for originality and creativity in the sense of spontaneous creation. For Skinner, uniqueness is the product of genetic and environmental histories, as we have seen. Skinner explains change by equating operant conditioning with natural selection in the sense that they both depend on the appearance of "mutations" (random changes) for any kind of change. The "good" for Skinner is what survives, as in natural selection. Thus Skinner, like the Darwinians, is able to explain the millions of species of life on earth without recourse to a creative mind. In a similar way, Skinner argues, the contingencies of reinforcement explain how science and art have come about without appealing to man's creativity or dynamism. In *Walden Two*, where all the contingencies of reinforcement are arranged, Skinner assures us that the arts and sciences flourish. We will consider his argument further in the discussion of the novel.

Does Skinner Rely Too Much on Animal Behavior?

Some critics argue that the rats and pigeons the Behaviorists work with do not reflect the human condition, and that any predictions of human behavior on the basis of such experiments are limited only to those characteristics which human beings share with animals. The differences between men and animals, Skinner's critics point out, are not simply quantitative but qualitative. Arguing from animals to man is therefore highly unreliable. One critic of Skinner has coined the term "ratomorphism" to refer to the practice of applying the characteristics of animal behavior to man. Skinner's response, briefly, is this: Experimental analysis of behavior is no longer restricted to rats and pigeons; many species including man are being studied today. Furthermore, all science moves from the simple to the complex, and there are, after all, many features which men and animals share even though man may have more complex "repertoires of behavior." Finally, the science of behaviorism has established that all animals including man are subject to laws governing behavior, that all change behavior under the influence of reward and consequences of behavior.

Is Skinner's Approach Naive?

There are those critics who insist that Skinner's approach to human behavior is naive and intellectually bankrupt. Arthur Koestler has dismissed Skinner's psychology as a "monumental triviality." Skinner's response is that critics who take this view usually do not fully understand his psychology. They labor under various misunderstandings: that Skinner reduces behavior to stimulus-response, that in Skinner's view people are just like rats, etc. It is the mentalistic explanations, Skinner counters, that are actually oversimplified, because they explain nothing. Attributing behavior to the Oedipus complex or to general feelings of anxiety, is, for Skinner, an evasion of explaining behavior. And besides, Skinner points out, if his psychology were as trivial as his critics say it is, then why do they spend so much energy attacking it? This fact Skinner interprets as a sign of the vitality of his science.

Does Skinner Dehumanize Man?

Other critics insist that operant conditioning dehumanizes man since it includes no theory of man and therefore sees behavior without the behaving person. As they see it, Skinner neglects the most important human attributes: choice, intention, creativity, morality. All these attributes, according to Skinner, can be explained by behavioral analysis, for no human feature is beyond it, not even morality. The criticism centers again on the question of human autonomy: Is man the author of his destiny or is he shaped by the environment? Although Skinner states that man is the product of his environment, he also suggests that man can construct and design the world in such a way as to increase freedom from constraint and to extend human possibilities. Making a list of all the threats and dilemmas men face today -

nuclear war, pollution, over-population, racial discrimination, exploitation of the world's resources - Skinner insists that these conditions can be remedied, but only if we recognize the supreme influence of the environment and learn to manage and control ourselves and our world more effectively. To do this must dismiss the notion that morality and justice are personal possessions and begin to analyze the contingencies that have shaped our systems of government, our religions, our economic systems, etc. It is these contingencies we must understand if we are to build a world in which people behave morally and justly.

Is Operant Conditioning Totalitarian?

Some critics feel that operant conditioning is a dangerous technique for controlling others and thus a dangerous tool for totalitarianism. Skinner recognizes and acknowledges that his techniques can be and are exploited by powerful governments and religions to manipulate and control others. Arranging contingencies in order to shape behavior is certainly manipulative, but not necessarily exploitative, Skinner argues. At any rate, not arranging contingencies (leaving them to chance) also shapes behavior, often with undesirable consequences. Skinner seems to have a point here. To say that all control is wrong is a failure to face up to the issue. Control is important and unavoidable in education, government, therapy, and elsewhere. Skinner does not, however, face up to all the ramifications of the problem of power, as we shall see when we discuss this problem in *Walden Two*.

Does Science Destroy the Mystery?

Finally, there is the criticism that Skinner's specific analysis of behavior removes the mystery and the inexplicable characteristics of human beings. This does not seem to be a very sound argument against Skinner since there is little to be gained by defending human behavior as capricious or totally unpredictable. Nor should Skinner be reprimanded for trying to improve our understanding of human behavior.

ASSESSMENT OF WEAKNESSES IN SKINNER'S PSYCHOLOGY

In our general criticism of Skinner we have tried to reflect accurately and fairly the kinds of arguments that are often made against him. Skinner is, of course, aware of these arguments and has tried to refute them on a number of occasions. Whatever one may conclude about the validity or invalidity of each argument, there are two overriding issues concerning Skinner's claims that require special attention. All of Skinner's confident assertions should, of course, be subject to scrutiny and critical examination.

Skinner's Rejection of "Mentalistic" Approaches

The first of these objections has to do with Skinner's offhanded and crude rejection of all mentalistic explanations of human behavior. When Skinner states that the mentalistic approach to man has resulted in no concrete knowledge about human behavior and that 2,000 years of reflective thought has produced nothing worthwhile, he is either incredibly naive or simply distorting things in favor of his own analysis. To insist, as Skinner does, that speculation about consciousness as a form of self-knowledge from Plato to the phenomenologists has been a complete waste of time is a form of arrogance that boggles the mind. One must keep in mind that this kind of gross generalization sweeps away with one fell swoop Socrates, Christ, Augustine, Shakespeare, Kant, Hegel, Marx, Goethe, Sartre, etc.

Skinner's Sweeping Claims

While proclaiming the general decline and uselessness of the mentalistic approach, Skinner claims all kinds of results for his own experimental analysis. These claims, however, are generally unsubstantiated. He claims, for instance, that there exists already an "effective technology" which will ultimately demonstrate that human behavior is completely a function of environment. It would seem fair to say that at the present moment at least the question still remains open. Many of the applications of operant conditioning seem to many people to be little more than common sense. Clearly, operant conditioning does explain a great deal of our habitual behavior. But can Skinner's scientific analysis is behavior really explain such complex behavior as creating poetry? sculpture? philosophy? The reinforcement contingencies in this kind of behavior would seem to be beyond measurable, observable activity and hence beyond the explanatory power of operant conditioning. All behavior that involves thought, imagination - any behavior, in fact, that is not directly observable - presents innumerable difficulties for a science of human behavior based on direct observation.

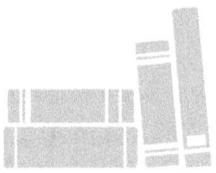

WALDEN TWO

WALDEN TWO AND THE UTOPIAN TRADITION

Walden Two is a novel about a modern utopian community based on Skinner's science of human engineering, especially on the possibilities inherent in positive reinforcement. Skinner's motivation for designing his utopia is traditional: he begins with the basic recognition that there is great disparity in the world between what is real and what is possible. What is real, outside of Walden Two, is a world of poverty, strife, despair. There are affluence and luxury, but there are also their opposites. It is the world Burris describes while taking a walk at the end of the novel: squalor, hopelessness, desperation, the empty humanism of the latest version of the speech given annually by the president of his university. All this is contrasted with life inside Walden Two, where life is portrayed as richly rewarding and rational.

Skinner's optimistic view of the good life comes at a time when utopian thinking has generally declined. This decline is evident in such famous 20th Century anti-utopias as Huxley's *Brave New World*, Orwell's *1984*, Zamiatin's *We*. These anti-utopias or "dystopias" reflect a general disillusionment with and revulsion against utopian thinking. Today utopia is equated in many people's minds with empty idealism, impracticality, and folly. *The Oxford English Dictionary* lists two contradictory definitions for the word "utopia": a) "a place, state, or condition ideally perfect in respect of politics, laws, customs, and conditions," and b) "an impossibly ideal scheme, especially for social improvement." Most people today associate utopia with the latter definition.

This negative attitude toward utopia has developed at a time when many people think that new utopian visions are more necessary than ever before. Anti-utopianism is seen by some to be a troublesome and unproductive attitude.

For one thing, it involves anti-social tendencies, as George Kateb points out in his book *Utopia and Its Enemies* (1963); it threatens to deprive us of any reasonable hope for a better future, at a time when keeping such hopes alive is important; and, as Karl Mannheim emphasizes in his book *Ideology and Utopia* (1936), a society without any utopian elements tends to stagnate and become one-dimensional, ultimately to petrify.

In view of this 20th Century aversion toward utopian designs, Skinner faces a hostile audience to begin with. Certainly, some of the criticism of *Walden Two* reflects this general hostility toward utopia per se. In order to judge Skinner's utopian vision on its own merits, we should try to distinguish what in the criticism of *Walden Two* is contemporary bias against utopia and what are the particular shortcomings of Skinner's own vision. In order to place this problem in its proper perspective, we will begin by listing the most frequent attacks on utopian thinking as such.

20TH CENTURY AVERSION TO UTOPIAN THINKING

Many critics argue against utopia on the basis of recent history. Recent events - two World Wars, Auschwitz, Hiroshima - indicate that there are still dangerous furies within man that make any notion of utopia pure folly. These recent **catastrophes** prove that man still lusts for blood and is a long way from any kind of utopia. (One could argue, of course, that these recent **catastrophes** make new visions and designs for a better world even more urgent.)

Some people cite the historic outcome of Marxism and the general disillusionment with the dictatorship in Russia as an argument against utopia. Marxism in Russia did not lead to "the full and free development of every individual," as Marx claimed it would, but rather demonstrated the dangers inherent in utopian speculation.

Often critics reject utopia on the basis that proposed utopias have seldom been democracies. Utopias are usually ruled by an elite that rejects democratic institutions. Hence, utopia has become synonymous with totalitarianism. (We will consider later Frazier's reasons for rejecting democracy.)

Since all utopias are more or less planned societies, they are considered a threat to the values of freedom. Utopian societies are seen as fixed and closed, incapable of further development since in theory they have reached perfection. Even the "dynamic" patterns for utopia that stress change and progress do not allow for a basic change in organization. Frazier attempts to defend Walden Two against this charge, arguing that Walden Two is dynamic and progressive.

A common criticism is that utopia eliminates the intensity and variety of human experience by leveling out individual differences, reducing contrasts and oppositions, and in general making life dull, gray, and dreary. By eliminating such human experiences as anxiety, suffering and despair it somehow reduces man and diminishes the fullness and richness of life. The texture of life in utopia is found wanting. By stressing equality, utopia eliminates individuality, and individuality is seen as good thing.

Another frequent concern of the anti-utopian is the whole question of human malleability. Utopian psychology in general, and Skinner's psychology in particular, sees human nature as easily changeable. This becomes, however, a mixed blessing. On the one hand, it implies that human nature is plastic and can easily be changed for the better; on the other hand, it is frightening to realize that man is easily manipulated. The anti-utopians would like to maintain a sense of aura and mystery enshrouding man so that he will always be beyond full understanding and comprehension.

All these attitudes go a long way in explaining the contemporary lethargy in projecting new visions and designs for a better world. They should be kept in mind as we begin to evaluate Skinner's own aspiration for a better world, an aspiration that infuses *Walden Two* with a certain vitality and urgency.

A SHORT HISTORY OF UTOPIAN THINKING

All utopian thinking is essentially an expression of its own time. But each utopian design, to be fully understood, must be read within the utopian tradition. It is important to understand how Skinner's utopia reflects a development from previous utopian designs. A short history of utopian thinking will provide us with an overview of this rich tradition and will enable us to better judge and evaluate Skinner's *Walden Two*. How does Skinner improve on previous designs? Where does he build on previous concepts? Does *Walden Two* represent progress in utopian thinking or does it represent its ultimate decline?

While the term "utopia" does not appear in Plato's *Republic,* this work is generally considered to be the great archetype of all subsequent utopian designs. Many readers today see the *Republic* as the first blueprint for a totalitarian society. Plato's ideal society is static, maintains a stratified class system, relies heavily on strict censorship that extends even to music, practices eugenics, does away with the family as we know it, and places a great deal of importance on education (some would call it conditioning). Plato's "good community" is based on function or specialization, providing each man with an essential function to perform in order to have a healthy and disciplined society. It is modeled on the Greek city-state and ruled by a Philosopher-King.

Thomas More first coined the term "utopia" in 1516 to designate a place that does not exist. "Utopia" actually means "nowhere" in the sense that no such place actually exists on the map. More's *Utopia* describes a society on a fictional island, 2,000 miles long, with fifty-four large, well-planned cities within walking distance of one another. Inhabitants work approximately six hours each day, property is owned communally, and the family is kept intact. The general picture is one of a benevolent society, stressing humanistic education, religious tolerance, and natural reason. All money is abolished (chamber pots are made of gold), and "Utopia" seems less primed for war and competition than Plato's Republic. During the period of the Renaissance, there were a great many other projections of "the good place," many inspired by More, others following the pattern set down by Francis Bacon in the first technological utopia, *The New Atlantis* (1629). These Renaissance visions of utopia shared certain characteristics: they valued some form of democracy, sought to improve the political and social organization of society, stressed the importance of communal ownership of property, and sought to limit work to six or eight hours per day.

In the 17th Century, there was a definite decline in utopian thinking. Scholars point out that this century, the age of absolutism and the counter-Reformation, did not inspire literature with utopian elements. The utopian literature that was written tends either to reflect the totalitarian character of the time, or to find utopia on some far-off, idyllic island, away from the turmoil and chaos of civilization.

With the 18th Century, utopian writings were no longer set on a far-off island, but rather became models for social improvement in a recognizable present setting. Many of the ideals of the French Revolution reflected utopian concepts and expectations. The leaders of the French Revolution held divergent ideals, but they all demanded change, demanded, in fact, a complete transformation of society. Utopian demands centered again on communal ownership of property, abolition of exploitation and a more equitable distribution of wealth, improved governmental administration - all contained in the demand for liberty, equality, fraternity. Many of the values of the Enlightenment - belief in the natural rights of man, belief in justice, reason and tolerance - were incorporated in these utopian writings.

Even though the French Revolution failed to realize these values, they remained vital and alive and were eagerly embraced by 19th Century utopian writers. The 19th Century generated more utopian works than had ever before been written. Inspired by the progress in science and technology, these writers portrayed various possibilities for ideal socialist and communist states. Most of these visions were socialist-oriented:

communal ownership of the means of production was seen as the best safeguard against the exploitation inherent in the new technological society. One could make an imposing list of utopian writers of this period which would include Saint-Simon, Fourier, Bellamy, Hertzka, Morris, Wells and many others. Attempts were also organized to set up utopian communities such as the famous Oneida communities, Icarias, and New Harmony in the United States. Because of their smallness and their isolation from the rest of society, these attempts ultimately failed.

By the end of the 19th Century, many people were already developing a strong aversion to the socialist utopias. Karl Marx, although he had accepted many of the utopian proposals in his own system, severely criticized the utopian socialists. For Marx, they weren't scientific enough and rigorous enough in their analysis of society and their criticisms. Many others began to see the utopian socialists as naive and juvenile in their judgments of human nature.

In the 20th Century, the concept of social utopia has diminished to an intellectual abstraction. Although there are still a few utopian writers around, they are generally labeled unrealistic or absurd. The main thread of the utopian tradition is continued today in science-fiction writings in which all imagination is expended in devising technological fantasies. Those writers still concerned with genuine utopian values, e.g., Herbert Marcuse and Paul Goodman, are generally disregarded although they do have some followers. The anti-utopianism of our time can be measured by the fact that almost everyone has read or knows about Huxley's antiutopia, *Brave New World*, whereas few people are familiar with his positive utopian novel, *The Island*, a challenging image of utopia that seeks to combine the best aspects of Western science and technology with Eastern contemplative life.

During the turbulent 1960s however, there seemed to be a renewed interest in social utopias among the "counterculture" movements - communes, Hippie families, The Diggers, etc. Some of these were back-to-nature movements, but some were committed to qualitative changes in the future. More recently, social scientists and political theorists expressed renewed interest in the creative function of utopian thinking in terms of alternative possibilities for the future.

WALDEN TWO AS UTOPIA

We are now better able to see how *Walden Two* fits in with this varied tradition of utopian writing. In defending his utopian community, Frazier makes frequent reference to previous utopian designs, usually to point out how his community has solved former problems through the science of human engineering. One thing is clear from the outset: Walden Two is only a small, isolated community of about 1,000 members. Such small communities have proved unsuccessful in the history of utopias. And one wonders just how seriously one should take Skinner's community in terms of its overall applicability. There is one immediately apparent limitation to Skinner's ideal community: it is possible only within a limited community. For one thing, there simply aren't enough behavioral psychologists in the world to scientifically control the contingencies of reinforcement for a large population. This may prove a severe handicap in Skinner's utopian vision.

It is apparent that Skinner continues many traditional utopian values. The emphasis in Walden Two is on an enriching communal life; property is held and worked in common; children are brought up communally; work has been reduced to approximately four hours per day. Frazier defines the good life in traditional utopian terms: health, satisfying leisure, rewarding personal relationships, the happiness of the utopian membership. In Walden Two, there is complete equality of men and women, and, seemingly, ample opportunity to develop individual talents and potentials. In general, life in Walden Two is neither permissive nor rigidly regimented. In some respects Walden Two is critical of our consumer-oriented society and claims to have minimized the need for material goods and for variety, as well as for individual aggression and competition.

It is also apparent that Walden Two differs in one important respect from previous utopian designs: the science of human engineering. In the methods of human engineering Frazier thinks he has discovered the tool that will allow Walden Two to succeed where all previous attempts at utopian communities failed. This major innovation of Walden Two aims at the systematic conditioning of its inhabitants based on the benign principle of positive reinforcement. It is this innovation that is at the heart of the dispute over *Walden Two*. The aim of Frazier's "science," as he admits, is to eliminate the individual's struggle within himself, his personal anxiety and frustration, and to replace it with habitual observance of the community's standards. Members of Walden Two, because they have been scientifically conditioned, want to do only that which is good in community's eyes, and will perform whatever is required of them without strain or effort. It is this major innovation that we must now consider in some detail before we can come to general conclusions about Skinner's utopian vision. We will return to the question of Skinner's utopian vision: Is Skinner's vision bold and imaginative? Does it enhance or detract from human possibilities? Does *Walden Two* inspire us with a new image of man? What human energies does *Walden Two* liberate? Or does it glorify the ant-hill image of man?

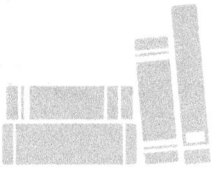

WALDEN TWO

STRATEGIES, THEMES, ISSUES - PART 1

Skinner skillfully introduces his main **themes** by setting up a situation that naturally motivates six people to visit a utopian community set up by one T. E. Frazier and called Walden Two. The narrator, Professor Burris (notice the intentional similarity to Skinner's own first name) is delineated as someone who has failed to find personal meaning and fulfillment in his profession as a teacher. The two veterans, Rogers and Jamnik, are characterized as looking for a more rewarding life based on cooperation and meaningful human relations. Augustine Castle is a valuable addition to the cast because as a philosophy professor interested in abstract speculations on utopias, he can be counted on to raise fundamental theoretical questions. The addition of Rogers' and Jamnik's girlfriends, Barbara and Mary, guarantees that the position of women will not be overlooked by male investigators. The visit of these six to Walden Two assures us that life inside Walden Two will be continuously contrasted with life outside the experimental community: that is, life as the reader knows it. Such contrast, explicit and implicit, is one of the main functions and aims of all utopian literature.

OVERALL STRATEGY OF WALDEN TWO

Before we consider some of the characteristics of this experimental community we must look at the overall strategy on which Walden Two operates. This strategy is outlined in the beginning of the novel by Rogers, who has read Frazier's article in which the general arguments for the institution Walden Two are set forth. These arguments are: A) Political action is not an effective means of improving society. Since politics lacks the precision of a scientific, experimental approach, politicians can only guess at solutions and this is a haphazard and inefficient way of shaping general policy. B) Modern technology has, however, reached a stage at which it can supply the necessary economic stability and leisure time to liberate people from the drudgery and debilitating labor that hampered earlier attempts at utopia. And most importantly, C) The principles of "behavioral engineering" can solve the problems that arise in any attempt at communal living. Most of Frazier's discussion is concerned with explaining precisely what behavioral engineering involves.

An introduction to the principles of "behavioral engineering" is immediately provided by the example of the portable electric fence which was initially employed in Walden Two to control the movement of a flock of sheep. Presumably, each time one of the original sheep came into contact with the fence, it received an electric shock. Frazier states that they soon discovered that the electric fence could be replaced by a piece of string which had the same effect. Furthermore, many of the sheep that had never been subjected to the shock tended to remain within the flock. Frazier mentions, however, that there is a sheepdog (named "Bishop") who maintains a watchful eye over the flock.

The electric fence is clearly an example of aversive conditioning since it involves pain, and even the string involves the threat of pain. The ineffectiveness of this kind of control is made abundantly clear in Chapter 34 when the sheep break out of their enclosure. Frazier states that this kind of control is based on a "primitive principle," i.e., force, threat, punishment. This kind of control may work for a while, as long as the sheep dog, Bishop, maintains a watchful eye. But without Bishop, Frazier states, "it would scarcely work at all." Even the later generation, which is not subjected to the shock, is not reinforced positively but, rather, negatively, and hence their behavior remains unpredictable.

The "revolt" of the sheep offers a clear-cut example of the shortcomings of punishment and negative reinforcement as methods of shaping behavior. This experiment (and we must remember that in Walden Two there is "a constantly experimental attitude toward everything") is completely misunderstood by Professor Castle, who sees it as "the revolt of the angels!" Actually the example of the sheep provides a parallel to the way in which behavior is controlled outside Walden Two. This is made evident in the course of the many conversations in which Frazier makes distinctions between the way behavior is shaped outside Walden Two and the scientific, experimental methods used within Walden Two.

In Frazier's analysis of the world outside Walden Two, the educational system, the political system, and all other institutions function on the principle of aversive control. And this control, Frazier says, is in the hands of charlatans, demagogues, and salesmen who use these techniques for their own self-interest and personal gain in a competitive world. Not only are these techniques inefficient and wasteful of human energy, they also go a long way in explaining our bloody history, the general neurosis in the outer world, the anxiety, suppressed behavior, and deviant behavior. The implications of this analysis, then, are far-reaching indeed.

Inside Walden Two these methods are replaced by a scrupulously thorough process of conditioning based on the principle of positive reinforcement. This process begins with the control of infant behavior and continues into the psychological management of the adults. Babies in Walden Two are brought up communally under controlled conditions designed to eliminate completely the experiences of fear, frustration, and anxiety. Hence, Frazier assures us, such emotions as anger, jealousy, envy and resentment are unknown in Walden Two. This is accomplished through the gradual introduction of obstacles and annoyances into the child's environment so that he learns how to cope with disappointments gradually at his own level. Throughout this process, force, threat, and punishment are expressly rejected.

Through a complicated series of schedules of reinforcement, each child is brought along at his own pace. Frazier's goal is to fit each individual for the frustrations and difficulties of life so that all become strong, capable of a "courageous" existence, not just the few "hardy children" who survive the accidental processes of traditional education. The ultimate aim, according to Frazier, is to teach each child self-control. Hence the infamous "lollipops" and bowls of "Forbidden Soup" that outrage Professor Castle. The lollipop experiment is designed to reward behavior which is capable of postponing gratification. Although Professor Castle refers to this as "sadistic tyranny," the methods, Frazier assures us, are benign, without recourse to punishment or threat.

The "tremendous power" which Frazier has discovered in behavioral engineering is positive reinforcement. Through experimental application of this power he is able to increase the probability of certain kinds of behavior and eliminate others. Unlike punishment, which breeds resentment and anxiety, positive reinforcement allows for the kind of control that allows the controlled to "feel free" even though their behavior is completely controlled. Crucial to Frazier's system of control is the careful designing of the environment - without this he could not control the contingencies of reinforcement. Through careful control of the environment, Frazier argues, human behavior can be controlled.

The overall strategy of Walden Two, then, is to do away with punishment, fear, threat, coercion (with all aversive conditioning), and to replace these techniques with positive reinforcement. This will result in perfect behavior in the sense that those who have undergone the complete conditioning processes of Walden Two will want to do only what they have been conditioned to see as beneficial to the individual and to the community. Furthermore, they will perform whatever is required of them without strain, anxiety or frustration. The methods of positive reinforcement ensure that there is no cause for revolt since there is no feeling of restraint. Unlike the sheep in their enclosure, the inhabitants of Walden Two allegedly have no reason to revolt.

CONDITIONING VS. EDUCATION

Much of the criticism of *Walden Two* is directed against the overall strategy we have been discussing. Many critics are appalled at its systematic conditioning of people. Some question whether the inhabitants of Walden Two have any self-awareness, any power of self-determination, any capacity for personal growth, any real character. These critics usually assume that our present system of education, with all its shortcomings, at least teaches people to think for themselves. We will have to consider this argument concerning the differences between conditioning and education before making a judgment on this question.

Frazier's position on conditioning is clear enough and may be paraphrased as follows: since all men are conditioned anyway (whether they face up to it or not), why not replace the usual methods of conditioning, which are capricious, unscientific and biased, for a planned, rational, efficient system of scientific control? To establish the ends toward which behavior ought to be shaped, Frazier asks two basic questions: "What is the best behavior for the individual as far as the group is concerned?" and secondly, "How can the individual be induced to behave in this way?" Once the answers to these questions are experimentally ascertained, the techniques of positive reinforcement will ensure the desired behavior.

In Frazier's view, then, there is no valid distinction between conditioning and education. All education is simply a form of conditioning, which aims at inculcating the values of a society into the individual. Every individual is ultimately "manipulated" by the contingencies of reinforcement to behave in a certain way. To put it simply, for Frazier conditioning is education, but it is a form of education that implies greater knowledge, awareness, and control of the contingencies of reinforcement, education in which less is left to chance. Conditioning is planning the environment and planning the schedules of reinforcement to increase the probability of the kind of behavior desired.

Frazier claims that his system produces happy, energetic people who are taught "techniques of learning and thinking." Critics of Walden Two think that Frazier's system does the opposite of teaching people to think; they feel that it deprives people of even the opportunity to think for themselves. If this is true, an inhabitant of Walden Two is little more than a mindlessly acting robot. These critics insist on a clear distinction between education and conditioning. Education, they say, aims at making the individual capable, self-reliant and self-directing.

They insist that education should increase self-understanding and understanding of the world so that the individual will be able to control himself better and choose his own goals in life. In brief, they argue that education should provide the individual with the knowledge and ability to shape his own behavior and character and to determine himself.

Clearly, such a view contains ideals and abstractions that the experimentally-minded Frazier cannot accept. For one thing, concepts such as self-determination or self-choice are antithetical to Frazier's entire system. For another, isn't it simply a fact that all education implies some conditioning, indoctrination and manipulation? Does our educational system actually train students in self-determination and self-choice? Frazier is challenging some of our most crucial assumptions about education, so we should probably consider his claims carefully instead of rejecting them out of hand. Frazier's view should motivate us to reconsider some of the ideals and unexamined assumptions that have become **cliches** in American education.

On the other hand, we should also critically examine Frazier's view. What are the implications of this kind of conditioning? Does it result in a mindless acceptance of the status quo? Will it, as Castle argues, replace conscious life with the life of the anthill? And more important, what about our notions of free choice, morality, individual responsibility? Can we still talk about man as a moral being if we accept Frazier's image of man?

We should not allow the benign depiction of positive reinforcement to obscure the image of man that lurks beneath Frazier's psychology. Some of the assumptions about human nature that Frazier makes become evident in his critical debate with Castle (Chapter 29). This debate centers around the freedom-determinism issue. Before we arrive at any evaluation of Frazier's methods of conditioning, we must consider this question in some detail, for in many respects it is the crucial question to ask about Walden Two.

FREEDOM VS. DETERMINISM

Frazier's position on the issue of freedom vs. determinism is, as he admits, "simple enough." He denies that freedom exists and claims that he must deny it or his entire system would be absurd: "You can't have a science about a subject matter which hops capriciously about." Like Skinner, Frazier admits that possibly it can never be proved that man is not free, but he claims that the successes of his utopian society make it difficult to believe that man is free. Repeatedly in his arguments with Castle, Frazier refers to the success of Walden Two as an accomplished fact, as a realization of the validity of his premises; but, of course, as readers we are aware that the entire community is a fiction. Nevertheless, the illusion created by Frazier's constant reference to the success of Walden Two is a beautiful example of behavioral engineering on Skinner's part.

Frazier's view on the freedom-determinism issue is precisely Skinner's own view as he has stated it in several contexts, including his book on the subject, *Beyond Freedom and Dignity*. There are two important aspects of this statement that we should emphasize before we embark on any further discussion of the subject. First, Frazier denies the reality of human freedom because, if man is free, then his entire science of human engineering is impossible; and secondly, Frazier admits that he cannot disprove the reality of human freedom. These important admissions make it clear that Frazier's science of behaviorism demands the assumption that man is completely knowable and predictable; in other words, Frazier assumes determinism.

Since this freedom-determinism issue is by Frazier's own admission the cornerstone of his science, we must try to place it in perspective so as to see all its ramifications. It is a question of central significance not only for *Walden Two*, but for Skinner's psychology as well. The freedom-determinism debate has been going on for centuries, both in the sciences and in the humanities. Although numerous books have been written on the subject, the question is a long way from being settled.

The central disagreement takes this form: those who argue for human freedom insist that our actions are to some extent a matter of choice. They argue that man is to some extent autonomous, and hence his actions can never be completely predictable. Those who argue for autonomous man point out that if man is completely shaped by physical forces, then such notions as human responsibility, morality, and integrity have no meaning. If man is simply a stimulus-response mechanism, if he is simply a robot or a marionette, then human life is irredeemably diminished and the human world is shattered.

For the determinist, on the other hand, all choice, decision, even the "feeling" of freedom, is an illusion. The determinist maintains that all causes of human behavior will one day be fully known, and then it will be clear once and for all that freedom and choice never existed. To a determinist like Frazier (and Skinner for that matter), autonomous man implies lawlessness, disorder, and unpredictability. Such a condition would make scientific analysis of behavior impossible since, if there is no cause-and-effect pattern in human behavior, there can be no scientific method of explaining that behavior. For Frazier, an image of man that "hops capriciously about" leads inevitably to philosophies of vitalism, mysticism and the occult - areas in which science has little relevance.

The freedom-determinism debate reached crisis proportions in the 19th Century in the struggle between religion and science. The findings of Darwin and Marx supported the view that man is essentially a part of nature and hence subject to its deterministic laws. Naturalist writers of the period argued that man is entirely shaped by his race, environment, and heredity, and demonstrated in their plays and novels the ineluctable powers of these forces. Even theology was affected as some leading theologians began to see Christ simply as a historical figure and God became merely a projection of man. These views have been challenged from time to time by philosophers and theologians who propose a more dynamic, vitalistic image of man.

Today in the field of psychology, the determinists seem to have prevailed (at least in America). Nevertheless, there is still profound disagreement among psychologists concerning the nature and quality of human volition. In psychology as in other fields, the protest against an all-embracing determinism is a recurring protest - an attempt to rescue man from the chains of matter and mechanism. Leading psychologists from the freedom camp (Maslow, Rogers) have debated this issue with Skinner and other behaviorists in order to bridge some of the disagreements, but it remains such a basic issue that it cannot be easily bridged. In Skinner's favor, we should remark that he is aware of how fundamental this issue is and has given a great deal of attention to it in his writings.

Comparison With Sartre

One way of bringing perspective to this issue is to compare Skinner's views with those of the French philosopher and writer Jean-Paul Sartre. Sartre's views on human liberty represent the polar opposite to Skinner's position. In his existential writings,

Sartre has repeatedly stated that man is "the author of himself" in the sense that man creates himself through his choices. Sartre's famous statement "existence precedes essence" means that man exists first and then chooses what he will become. In Sartre's radical view, the individual is free despite the deterministic findings of science. Heredity, environment, education, etc., on which Skinner bases his entire psychology, are for Sartre "explanatory idols" that explain nothing, but give the individual a convenient excuse for what he is. If one objects that heredity, history, environment certainly place limitations on my freedom, that my heredity, for example, determines my potentials, my capacities, etc., Sartre would agree that to exist means to exist "in situation," i.e., to exist within limiting conditions. But, for Sartre, man still retains free choice. Thus, I may be left-handed or right-handed, I may be handsome or ugly, it may be raining outside or sunny (these are things I can't change), but I am still master of these situations in the sense that I can adopt different attitudes towards them: I can accept them or adopt an attitude of revolt towards them or try to change them. Although I don't choose these conditions, I choose the way in which I will regard them, and hence I am free.

In extreme opposition to this view is Skinner/Frazier's pragmatic assumption of thoroughgoing determinism. This view maintains that man is moved by forces outside himself, and that through the experimental approach we can come to understand and control these forces. By arranging the environment benignly for man's benefit, the probabilities of human behavior can be predicted, and human behavior and human culture can be shaped for everyone's benefit. As we have seen, Skinner rejects the notion of a "inner-directed" man who gives himself his own attributes and qualities.

After Frazier states his pragmatic position on determinism, Castle replies that the ultimate test for freedom is "the experience of freedom," and he accuses Frazier of "bad faith" in his evasion of freedom. Frazier admits to a "feeling of freedom" - inhabitants of Walden Two, he says, "feel free" even though they are thoroughly conditioned. We have seen that the techniques of positive reinforcement require deliberate planning, design, and control - nothing can be left to chance. Those who have been subject to operant conditioning in Walden Two may feel that "they are doing what they want to do." In actuality, however, what they want to do has been designated by "careful cultural design." Frazier concludes: "We control not the final behavior, but the inclination to behave - the motives, the desires, the wishes."

Later, in a conversation with Burris, Frazier reinforces his view: "Our members are practically always doing what they want to do - what they 'choose' to do - but we see to it that they will want to do precisely the things which are best for themselves and the community." And of course what is best for the individual and the group has been carefully designated. The "feeling of freedom" is simply an illusion, but Frazier's concession of the importance of the feeling of freedom suggests that it is a necessary illusion in Walden Two; that is, it seems that Frazier has found that a sense of freedom is necessary to keep the individual from despair, or possibly from revolt. Thus, Frazier grants that the feeling of freedom is a necessary pragmatic device, but there can be no doubt that in order for Frazier's system to work (and he assures us that it does work), freedom and choice cannot actually exist in Walden Two.

At the same time there is another usage of the word "freedom" which would make the average member of Walden Two more free than those outside. Freedom in the sense of "freedom from" would make Walden Two, in Frazier's words, "the freest place in the world." This is true in the sense that inhabitants of Walden Two are free from having to make their own choices. They are free in the sense that they do not suffer any coercion, and they are free from the anxiety and doubts that free choice implies. It is this kind of freedom that Frazier has in mind when he says that most people would rather "be free from the responsibility of planning." This "freedom from" is, for Frazier, genuine liberation since it frees the individual from toil, insecurity, and anxiety. Most people, Frazier argues, want this kind of freedom - the freedom from worrying and competing in a cut-throat society in exchange for some assurance that the community will provide a decent and secure existence.

This analysis of freedom and determinism raises additional crucial questions about Walden Two. One wonders how a complete determinist like Frazier would explain how he came up with such a self-conscious plan of conditioning as is evident here. More importantly, the issue seems to divide the community into classes: those that are conditioned and those that are doing the conditioning. This explains why Frazier rejects democracy, and confronts us with the problem of a ruling elite and the necessity of safeguards against the abuse of power in Walden Two. We will examine these and related questions later in this chapter. First we must consider the implications of Frazier's determinism as they relate to ethical questions.

ETHICAL IMPLICATIONS

We have observed how the major innovation of Walden Two leads to the careful conditioning of behavior, to socially "correct" behavior. To ensure this, scrupulous care is taken in shaping behavior during the early, formative years. The importance of these early years is evident in the extreme care taken in controlling the environment in the Walden Two nurseries.

Temperature and humidity are carefully regulated; the baby is placed in a soundproof, germ-free compartment; even blankets and diapers are removed to prevent unpleasant, irritating experiences. Then, through carefully designed tolerance-building techniques, the "meaner and more annoying" emotions are extinguished from the child's repertoire of behavior. Children are never punished; only "good" behavior is rewarded. The techniques of positive reinforcement, Frazier claims, ensure that the child will be tolerant, cooperative and considerate. In fact, these techniques are so effective that Frazier can boast: "All our ethical training is completed by the age of six." In other words, by the age of six, every child in Walden Two behaves well entirely by habit. This means that every child will conform to the socially "correct" behavior without having to make an effort, without exertion.

Many readers of *Walden Two* find Frazier's statement curious. Some are puzzled by the statement that "ethical training" is something that can be completed at any age, much less at the age of six! Doesn't this kind of statement reveal Frazier's true intention, critics argue, which is to make people predictable computers? How can we have anything even remotely resembling ethical behavior if it occurs without continuous thought, reflection, and even some struggle with oneself? Doesn't ethical behavior necessarily imply human effort, human choice, and decision? Can ethical behavior ever become a mere habit?

It is important that we fully understand Frazier's argument on this issue. For Frazier, the important thing is not arguing in the abstract about the philosophical nature of ethics and morality, but rather that people be induced to do the "right thing" (in accord with what has been designated socially accepted behavior), and that they be able to do the right thing without strain, effort or struggle. Whether the behavior is automatic or the result of reflection and inner struggle is less important than the behavior itself. In fact, Frazier argues, wouldn't it be a great service to mankind to redeem people from all this inner struggle and turbulence and make it relatively easy for people to be good? Wouldn't it be more humane to make people do automatically what they ought to do anyway? Wouldn't this result in a more harmonious and balanced community with less stress and strain?

Frazier seems to have a valid argument on this issue. Certainly we would expect that in utopia it should be as painless as possible to be good. Frazier has already told us that the competitive values of the outside world have been removed in Walden Two, and replaced by values of cooperation, tolerance and mutual affection. This makes life less a pitched battle in which only the most aggressive and ambitious survive. As Frazier points out, outside Walden Two the luxury and wealth attained by some always implies the depravity and poverty of others. In such a world, the temptations for personal egotism and self-centered ambition are strong, and hence it is a struggle to be ethical. We agree that in utopia it should be easier to act morally.

Furthermore, there is a sense in which our moral behavior is shaped early in life. No one would deny that the ethical tendencies that we develop in childhood influence our later behavior in certain habitual activities. Even Sartre's existential analysis posits a "fundamental choice" usually made early in life, which influences subsequent choice. Hence, we can agree that much of our ethical behavior is shaped by a general pattern and does not require intense deliberation or soul-searching before each act.

Should Morality Involve Struggle?

Nevertheless, there are disturbing aspects to Frazier's elimination of effort from ethical behavior. Doing away with effort and striving seems to diminish the value of ethical behavior itself. Morality has traditionally been identified with conscious deliberation and individual struggle. It seems impossible, even in utopia, to make morality entirely a function of habit without irreparable damage to the traditional image of man as a moral agent. If ethical behavior is entirely automatic, then how do we recognize and measure moral achievement? Without some struggle between good and evil, between inclination and moral duty, between what we want to do and what we ought to do, there would be no moral consciousness.

This leads to perhaps the most serious criticism leveled against *Walden Two*, one that ought not be dismissed lightly. The question critics raise is this: do members of Walden Two have any moral consciousness at all? Do they have the capability of development and moral growth? Are they capable of continuous evaluation of their personal relationship with others in the community? It would seem that if all ethical training is completed by the age of six that ethical behavior has become completely automatic and hence stagnant. Even worse, automatic ethical behavior implies that members of Walden Two have no conscious awareness of why they are acting as they do. They cannot think of alternative ways of behaving, as their conditioning guarantees. And if members of Walden Two do not comprehend why they are acting as they do, then they are little more than mindless automatons, and Castle's analogy with the anthill seems appropriate. If this is the case, then activity in Walden Two, as critics have noted, degenerates into empty motions without thought, action without understanding and without consciousness. Even for those not born inside Walden

Two, Frazier states that "the Code acts as a memory aid until good behavior becomes habitual." But behavior that is only habitual, even if it is good behavior, does destroy the conception of man as a moral agent capable of moral excellence through his own effort. Sacrificing moral consciousness in favor of efficiency and habitual goodness is to sacrifice man as a moral creature, and would spell the end of conscious life.

Frazier disguises the full implications of this recognition with his humane and benevolent intentions. He wants to liberate men from the tensions and strain of acting ethically. He wants to lift from men the burden that moral behavior implies. By eliminating the tension between what man ought to do and what he wants to do, he relieves man of the responsibility of making his own choices. Leaving aside the question of whether this is possible or not, there should be no mistake about his intentions. Before we embrace Skinner's utopian community it is important that we recognize and reflect on these implications.

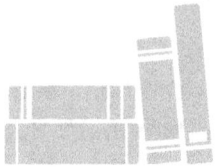

WALDEN TWO

STRATEGIES, THEMES, ISSUES - PART 2

....

POLITICAL DESIGN OF WALDEN TWO

The political organization of Walden Two is gradually made evident in Frazier's lengthy debates with Professors Castle and Burris. From these discussions emerges a political design that rests on two fundamental principles: 1) Experts and specialists dominate every field of human endeavor, and 2) Walden Two is a "world without heroes" in the sense that individuality, personal dominance, and the cult of personality have been successfully overcome, to the extent that even the expression of personal gratitude has been eliminated through cultural engineering.

Frazier tells us that the first plank of the Walden Two platform is that the "good life" cannot be obtained at all through politics and government because the techniques of government rely on the principles of force, threat, negative reinforcement, and hence are bad human engineering. Furthermore, the practices of politics are not based on scientific premises and therefore cannot exploit the possibilities of the experimental attitude. In Walden Two, on the other hand, politics is based on experimental findings which indicate the most efficient ways of getting things done.

The business of politics in Walden Two is therefore conducted by a group of specialists: The Planners and Managers. They are specialists who are attracted to long range goals and overall planning. There are six Planners (three men and three women who serve for ten years each) and numerous Behavioral and Cultural Managers (Manager of Personal Behavior, Manager of Cultural Behavior, Manager of Public Relations, Dairy Manager, Political Manager, Manager of Marriages, etc.). These Planners and Managers shape the general policy of the community and provide the direction in which Walden Two will move.

We have already observed Frazier's arguments against freedom and choice: most people, he claims, would rather give up the burden of planning and the uncertainty of making personal choices in favor of happiness and day-to-day contentment; most people prefer security to the ambiguity of freedom. Hence, Frazier is consistent in his rejection of democracy and democratic procedures and institutions. In Walden Two the general membership does not participate in government and politics. The task of government is assigned to a handful of specialists who are experts in the field. Frazier dismisses democracy as a "pious fraud," claiming that it is incongruous with the experimental spirit of a scientific society. Since most people have neither the expertise nor the special skills required in governing, how can they make a judgment, Frazier asks - especially in national campaigns in which issues are generally obscured by empty rhetoric and promises. In a democratic system, the electorate usually becomes the scapegoat of the politician, and Frazier argues that democracy ultimately leads to a despotism of the majority forcing its will on the minority.

Frazier's critique of democracy centers mainly around the incredible waste and inefficiency of the system.

By contrast, all decisions of importance in Walden Two are made by Planners and Managers, who consequently constitute the elite of the community. Frazier assures us, however, that they do not constitute a privileged class since they work in complete anonymity. To prevent the abuse of power, they receive no special treatment and no disproportionate share of the community's wealth. Their powers are further limited since they can't compel anyone to do anything - members of Walden Two select their own work. In addition, the sense of history is discouraged (in fact, history is not taught in Walden Two) to prevent the development of individual heroes or special regard for individual distinction. All personal skill and individual strength is de-emphasized in the cooperative culture of Walden Two. A further safeguard against the abuse of power is the fact that there is no concentration of power in Walden Two - there is no military or police machinery. And perhaps most significant, in Walden Two all aggressive urges and will to power are extinguished through a carefully designed educational process based on positive reinforcement.

Threat Of Absolutism

In spite of all these assurances, Frazier seems to understate the potential power of this group of Managers and Planners. It is they, after all, who will decide what kind of behavior will be reinforced and what kind discouraged. When we add to this fact the function of the Walden Two Code, the picture that emerges is somewhat disquieting. The Code prescribes rules of conduct for Walden Two members. It contains such significant rules as prohibiting members of the community from discussing the

Code in public and descends to such harmless social rules as not waiting for an introduction before speaking to someone and the free expression of boredom. The important thing to note, however, is that the Code cannot be discussed with the membership at large and that the rules of the Code can only be changed by the Managers and Planners. This seems to give the Managers and Planners almost absolute power in determining the fate of Walden Two.

In order to dispel any resemblance between the machinery of power within Walden Two and the totalitarian system of Soviet Russia, Frazier also provides a critique of the Russian system. Although the Russian experiment started with humanitarian impulses, Frazier feels that it quickly degenerated to the level of power politics. For one thing, the Russians lost sight of the experimental spirit; their use of propaganda is self-limiting and distorting. Furthermore, they developed a "cult of heroes," and politics cannot become a science so long as it requires a Lenin or Stalin to maintain it. But more importantly, Russia still relies on the tactics of power, which implies force, threat, etc. Since they have not mastered the cultural-engineering techniques of positive reinforcement, they are a long way from inducing people to behave "freely" for their mutual welfare.

The overall effect of the distribution of power in Walden Two is to make the political function of the community just like any other function insofar as it, too, is carried on by specialists. Some people would question whether the political function is just like any other function. We tend to admire the expert in science, medicine, technology, but deeply distrust him in the field of politics. "Power corrupts and absolute power corrupts absolutely" is a familiar slogan that implies that in the world of politics there must be a carefully designed system of checks and balances. Many people think that the expert in politics, because of the nature of his specialty, requires careful supervision and control by the electorate to prevent abuses.

Many critics dismiss Frazier's utopian community because of his out-and-out rejection of democracy. They argue, like Castle, that this makes the members of Walden Two less than full citizens, reduced to objects in the hands of the Managers and Planners. Since the members cannot discuss the Code by which, after all, they lead their lives, there is some question as to whether they fully comprehend their own system. Frazier tries to assure us that there is no cause for concern since all the trappings of power are absent from Walden Two. One can't help wondering, though, whether these happy, energetic people really understand how their own society works. Furthermore, all this emphasis on function and specialization seems to make a virtue out of fragmentation. Instead of nurturing the "whole man," Walden Two is consciously designed to produce narrow specialists who do not understand each other. Only the elite group of Planners and Managers has an overall view of the community. And one would expect, especially in utopia, that each individual member should have a clear understanding of the community in which he lives.

CHANGE

After discovering that Walden Two is the result of Frazier's "grand plan" and that Frazier remains the guiding genius behind it, Castle asserts that intellectually Walden Two is a dead end and draws an analogy to the beehive. Like the beehive, Castle claims, Walden Two is incapable of spontaneous change. Frazier admits that his community is predetermined, but he claims that intellectually it will continue to develop and change no matter how much intelligence in shaped by the educational system.

This seems, at first sight, an important concession by a determinist like Frazier. But obviously it does not mean that the average member of Walden Two is free to overthrow the master plan, which conditions a function for intelligence as it does for everything else. The carefully designed techniques of behavioral engineering make certain of that. Intelligence seems "free" only to the extent that its function is encompassed within the master plan.

Nevertheless, Frazier insists throughout his discourse that Walden Two is a progressive community capable of change. In fact, he claims that this capability for change is what distinguishes his community from past utopian attempts and insures its survival value. Past communities suffered from the fatal defect - they lacked a future dimension and hence ultimately stultified and stagnated. In Walden, by contrast, there is "an active drive toward the future."

It is startling to hear Frazier talk about change in *Walden Two* for two reasons: first of all, the premises of a science of human behavior are based on systematic conditioning which would, at least on the surface, rule out the possibility of change. Frazier's views on freedom and democracy certainly run counter to the whole idea of change. Secondly, the concept of utopia implies in most people's minds a static society with built-in safeguards against change. After all, if utopia implies perfection, why change?

We can only conclude that Frazier's emphasis on change underscores his desire to see his community as dynamic and open-ended and, at the same time, completely planned. Walden Two, he claims, is capable of growth and development with time. This will give his community the capability of survival in a continually changing world; as man's needs, desires, and wishes change, Walden Two will be able to encompass those changes.

From what he have observed within Walden Two, it would be difficult to make a case for it as a dynamically changing community. Nowhere in Walden Two do we see any real mechanism for change. Change, as generally viewed, can only come about through tension, strife, disagreement; that is, through a dialectical relationship of opposites. But we have already seen that in Walden Two tensions and oppositions have been intentionally minimized, if not extinguished, in favor of efficiency and harmony. There is, of course, the emphasis on the experimental method. But the kind of experimentation that we see in Walden Two will only refine the basic assumptions on which Walden Two operates. This kind of experimentation can never lead to any radical change because of the basic assumptions of the science of human behavior. And if experimental evidence indicated the reality of human freedom, would the Planners of Walden Two be able or willing to incorporate the changes that would then be called for?

More significant with regard to change is Frazier's rejection of the study of history. We have seen that history, the record of human change and progress, is expressly outlawed in Walden Two. This is terribly ironic since history could possibly provide his community with an apparatus for change. It is, in fact, doubly ironic since Frazier's own community reflects the development and change from previous utopian patterns, and Frazier makes it evident from his many references to these utopias that he has obviously read and profited from them.

RELIGION AND THE FAMILY

Skinner's fictional community is entirely secular. As his spokesman, Frazier, points out: religious training is not part of the educational system in Walden Two. Since everything hinges on a scientific analysis of man, the supernatural, myths, revealed truth, and rituals are expressly rejected. Formal religious practices are almost nonexistent in Walden Two. The Sunday meetings that Frazier mentions are mainly therapy sessions in which music is played, and even though the Bible is read from time to time, it is valued mainly for the aesthetic and intellectual experience it affords. There are no priests or clergy in Walden Two. The psychologist has taken over the function of the priest in former times.

In Walden Two, human hopes are fulfilled here on earth, and hence religious faith has become pretty much irrelevant, as Frazier points out. Walden Two is clearly this-worldly in its orientation, and this characteristic places it within the mainstream of utopian thinking. In general, utopian thinkers do not seek another world, only a better world. The focus is not on the hereafter, but on the here and now, and as Frazier points out, the "good life" is possible here and now.

Another sacrosanct institution eliminated to a degree is the traditional concept of the family. We have observed that children are raised communally in Walden Two, thus striking down the nuclear family as the basic economic and social unit. Frazier's arguments for this change are reminiscent of Plato's *Republic* with the difference that in Walden Two parents know who their children are. Raising children communally, according to Frazier, eliminates all kinds of problems. In Walden Two, children are encouraged to view every adult as a parent (and vice versa). Hence, one could make an argument that Walden Two actually extends the family rather than limiting it. The terms "mother" and "father are discouraged in favor of first names; the work system actually allows each parent to spend more time with his/her child and with other children; and both men and women work in the nurseries. This last point is important because it prevent the situation in which one parent (usually the mother) is totally in charge of raising the child. Furthermore, the sharing of parental duties prevents one-sided identification of the child with either parent and liberates the child to select from a variety of models within the community.

In another utopian community, Huxley's *The Island*, the author achieves a similar purpose through the "Mutual Adoption Club," a group of fifteen to twenty-five couples in which everyone adopts everyone else's children. This provides each child with approximately twenty different homes, provides security, and allows the child in a sense to "choose" his own parents when disagreements develop with the biological parents.

The supervision of children is perhaps the most crucial function in Walden Two, and everyone in Walden Two takes an active interest in it. Since these early years are extremely significant in terms of human engineering, one wonders whether this supervision is actually carried out only by trained psychologists or whether every adult in Walden Two is expert enough to participate. In Frazier's description, the latter seems to be the case. One thing, however, becomes clear: the great care required in controlling "the contingencies of reinforcement" makes it evident that only a small number of children can be involved. Otherwise, a great number of behavioral psychologists would be needed to attend to the Walden Two nurseries.

Another important innovation in this regard is the relaxation of sexual standards. In Walden Two, young people get married at the age of sixteen or seventeen and usually have their first child at the age of eighteen. Having children early, Frazier claims, is not only good for the mother, but eventually liberates her from the burden of child-bearing by the time she is twenty-two and twenty-three years old. Although this may seem to be a radical feature, it is, as Burris notes, a practice that was quite common in former times and still is in many cultures. Barbara Macklin's incredible naivete concerning this practice only reflects her immaturity, her failure to develop beyond adolescence. It is clear that she is a product of the world outside Walden Two.

Role Of Women Is Enhanced

Perhaps the most appealing characteristic of Walden Two is the balancing of the sexes and the liberation of women from the fixed roles and oppressive tasks that society has traditionally imposed. In Walden Two the prescribed roles of women have changed. They enjoy complete economic and sexual independence. They are not seen as sex objects; in Walden Two, friendship is reinforced and the principle "Seduction not expected" is well-established. One would have to agree with Frazier that the role of woman in Walden Two is enhanced and made more dignified. All this, Frazier carefully notes, does not lead to promiscuity. This change in attitude toward women, as well as the changes in family structure, are all designed to promote a richer communal life. This situation involves changes from the way we are doing things now, but one has the feeling that these would be welcome changes.

"LABOR CREDITS"

Another interesting feature of Skinner's hypothetical utopia is the economic system. Since Walden Two does not operate on the profit system, there is a great deal of effort expended in making work a pleasant and personally rewarding experience. Members of Walden Two work for approximately four hours a day, for which they receive "labor credits." Since in theory everything is free in Walden Two, each member assumes his share of the burden of work for the goods and services he receives from the community as a whole. The value of these credits (approximately 1,200 per year) is arrived at by adjusting the value of a certain kind of work on the basis of demand: jobs that are less in demand receive higher value-ratings than jobs in great demand.

Everyone works in Walden Two, and Frazier assures us that everyone is free to select his own work. Even the Planners and Managers are required to do physical labor for one or two credits daily. This is obviously designed to keep them from developing the aura of an elite class. One wonders, however, just how free each member is to "choose" his own work in light of the claims Frazier has made for behavioral engineering.

Nevertheless, Frazier demonstrates to Castle that four hours of work within Walden Two is equivalent to more than eight hours of work outside Walden Two. This is accomplished through several innovations.

There is full employment in Walden Two. Everyone in Walden Two works for himself in the sense that each member has a stake in the community. Furthermore, there is no alienation of the worker from the product of his labor since he does not sell his labor for a wage. Hence the individual is more motivated, accomplishes more, and finds his work more fulfilling.

Work done in the first four hours of the day is more productive and efficient than that done later in the day when the individual grows tired and experiences tedium. Along the same lines, Walden Two relies on a great many labor-saving devices (e.g., the clear plastic trays and the large teacups) which minimize work. And the extremely efficient system of management and control in Walden Two prevents any duplication of effort.

Many of the jobs outside Walden Two have been completely eliminated. Generally these are jobs that are useless in terms of production - work in beauty parlors, insurance companies, department stores, the transportation industry, advertising, etc. These functions are all useless in Walden Two.

Perhaps most important is the liberation of women in Walden Two from the drudgery of "housewifery." Not only does this increase the work force considerably (by 50%), but, as Frazier points out, it is an immeasurable saving in human energy and vital spirits. To put this into perspective, all we need do is think of an average American neighborhood at about 5:30 in the afternoon. In every home there is a woman who is in the process of preparing the evening meal. Each one is expending energy in the duplication of the same process. Each serves the meal to her family and each washes up individually after the meal, using up enormous amounts of water and human energy. Savings in time, human effort, and natural resources are self-evident when we compare this wasteful system to the system in Walden Two, where there is communal dining and where the entire process has been mechanized to eliminate drudgery. Since meals are carefully planned ahead of time there is also less spoilage and waste of food. Also, we should note that food in Walden Two is not processed, packaged, and chemically sustained from spoiling. Since it is grown right there, it is harvested just prior to cooking; thus, it is fresh and high in vitamins and minerals that would otherwise be lost.

We should point out also that, although Walden Two is an agrarian community, it is highly mechanized and technologically developed. In fact, technology becomes a genuine force for liberation since, as Frazier points out, in Walden Two technology eliminates work, not the worker. The experimental spirit of the community ensures the continuous search for easier, more efficient ways of doing things in order to provide more leisure time for art, research, science - the enjoyment and enhancement of life.

CREATIVE ARTS

In his conversation with Burris toward the end of the novel, Frazier reveals his complete, messianic faith in his science of human behavior. In order to convince Burris to remain in Walden Two he speculates about the potentials that are inherent in his science. In comparison to his discovery, even the splitting of the atom pales, Frazier claims. He talks feverishly about pushing forward into new realms and confesses that his only genuine interest in Walden Two is in further developing his science (Walden Two provides him with a laboratory in which he can control the contingencies of reinforcement). In his enthusiasm, he talks about the total design of people to any set of specifications. Potentially, he claims, his science is capable of shaping better mathematicians, better musicians, better craftsmen and artists, and even better behaviorists. With brash confidence (somewhat embarrassing) he talks about constructing "groups of artists and scientists who will act as smoothly and efficiently as champion football teams."

In fact, the arts are already flourishing in Walden Two, to the extent that Frazier talks about a new Golden Age. Burris has been amazed in his wanderings through the passageways (which function as art galleries) at the many excellent paintings by Walden Two members. There seems to be great appreciation not only for art but for music and theatre as well. Frazier boasts of original compositions in music and even an original play. In Frazier's analysis of art, three important factors are necessary for the development of excellence in art forms: 1) sufficient leisure time, including freedom from worry about the material necessities of life, which are amply provided in Walden Two; 2) positive reinforcement through encouragement and reward from a nurturing environment, which, as we have seen, is the bulwark of Walden Two; and 3) the absence of financial or commercial barriers on the artist. In Walden Two the artist does not have to worry about appealing to an audience or placating commercial interests.

We are inclined to agree with Frazier that these conditions are important for the development of great art. Historical evidence reveals that art has flourished during periods of patronage which provided leisure and freedom of expression for the artist. And since the arts are presented as an accomplished fact in Walden Two, it is difficult to pass judgment. Nevertheless, we should also note that many theories of aesthetics stress the fundamental need for strife, tension, and suffering as prerequisites for the creation of art. Others insist at least on the necessity of a rich and varied experience to provide materials for artistic expression. According to these theories, the complete equanimity, harmony, and absence of struggle and tension in Walden Two could only produce bland, uninspiring art.

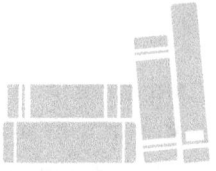

WALDEN TWO

CHARACTERIZATION IN WALDEN TWO

Characterization is not very complex in *Walden Two*, a feature shared by much utopian fiction. Usually, in utopian fiction, characters are simply mouthpieces for ideas or ideological positions. *Walden Two* is not much different, although the character of Frazier presents some interesting ambiguity and complexity.

T. E. Frazier is the founder of Walden Two and remains the guiding force behind the imaginary community. What strikes the reader about Frazier's personality is that, unlike those who were born in Walden Two (and subjected to lollipop training and bowls of Forbidden Soup), he is short-tempered, aggressive, and intolerant. He refers to himself as "a curious study of opposites," implying that, although he is responsible for the well-adjusted behavior of the people in Walden Two, he remains, paradoxically, a product of the world outside. He is certainly not a personable or likeable individual. Skinner has stated that he intentionally gave Frazier a "negative charisma." In comparison with the average member of Walden Two, he is a complete failure (he exhibits frustration, resentment, anger). His behavior accentuates the shortcomings and failures of life outside Walden Two.

Castle refers to him as the "primum mobile" (i.e., the first moving thing), a designation Frazier rejects. Nevertheless, Frazier is the one who set it all up and remains in power as one of the Planners who design the schedules of reinforcement. In spite of this power, Skinner takes great pains to point out that Frazier is no longer moving or directing things. He has successfully managed to suppress his leadership. Frazier assures us that Walden Two is a "world without heroes" and that the welfare of the community takes precedence over all else. To reinforce this we witness other members of Walden Two completely disregarding Frazier's wishes (they decide to go swimming instead of heeding his requests), and, as Burris discovers in his conversation with an elderly woman, some members don't even know who Frazier is. All this is designed to assure us that, although Frazier planned Walden Two as a "long-term experiment," he has managed to become quite anonymous and to blend in with the rest of the community.

Nevertheless, having set up the process of conditioning and character development in Walden Two, Frazier wields a god-like power, and at times he attributes god-like powers to himself. "I like to play God," he admits in his conversation with Burris, and, while overlooking "his creation" from his "throne" high on a hill, he says, "These are my children, Burris ... I love them." To underscore the power inherent in positive reinforcement, Skinner portrays Frazier with some ambivalence. After reassuring us that Frazier need not be feared, he invests him with a god-complex and exposes his dictatorial and arrogant nature. This adds an ambiguity to Frazier's character that should not be overlooked. Besides pointing to the awesome power of the science of behavior, it provides a distancing effect and keeps us from identifying with Frazier. This is important since many critics have identified Frazier's statements with Skinner himself, a reasonable judgment since many of Frazier's statements echo Skinner's views as reflected in his textbooks and other publications. We should recognize, however, that Skinner is detaching himself from Frazier's messianic personality and putting ironic distance between himself and his character.

Professor Burris, the psychologist and narrator of this account of Walden Two, should be identified more closely with Skinner's own position (we have noted that Skinner has given to this character a name similar to his own first name, Burrhus). Burris remains apprehensive of Frazier's godlike ambitions and tendencies, and at times satirizes the enthusiastic claims that Frazier makes. Throughout his stay in Walden Two, he attempts to remain aloof and critically detached from what he sees. He makes excursions on his own in order to gather valid and objective data on Walden Two. What appeals most to him about the community is the absence of governmental and bureaucratic interference in people's lives, what he calls its "Thoreauvian side." (Here he refers, of course, to the individual experiment in simplified living recounted in Thoreau's *Walden,* for which Frazier's community is named.)

It is through the character of Burris that the narrative achieves whatever tension it has. From the very beginning of his account, we know that Burris is discontented and dissatisfied, a man on the road to despair. He finds his teaching profession bothersome and unrewarding and has lost faith in himself and his research. He is indifferent and sarcastic about his role as a teacher and questions the efficacy of what he is doing. Through his own narrative we witness the rebirth of Professor Burris. After only a few hours outside Walden Two he becomes disgusted by the despair, the poverty, and the human hopelessness he sees all around him. He decides to return as a pilgrim, symbolic of his conversion to the ideals of Walden Two.

He has found a new commitment in his life and is convinced now more than ever that science can solve the social problems that caused his feelings of hopelessness. Burris' return to Walden Two at the end removes some of the narrative distance between himself and Frazier; nevertheless, he returns still apprehensive of Frazier. He glances up to Frazier's throne and notes with relief that Frazier is not there. Burris, the reader feels, will add a steadying and moderating effect to Frazier's extremist potential. Even though he returns, his suspicions of Frazier have not completely subsided.

Professor Augustine Castle, a Professor of Philosophy, functions mainly as Frazier's antagonist. Although he appears pompous and overbearing at times, he is, as Burris remarks, no "second rater." He is perceptive, intelligent, skeptical - all in all, a worthy opponent for Frazier, and like Frazier he is capable of expressing extreme positions. Satirized by Burris for his dedication to academia ("In his preoccupation with Mind, Castle had let himself put on too much weight"), Castle represents the liberal humanist's arguments against Frazier's scientific designs. Burris suspects him of Thomism. At any rate, Castle's final estimate of Frazier as "a modern, mechanized, managerial Machiavelli" and his suspicions that Frazier is "a tin god" are partially supported by Burris' own reservations.

Castle's own shortcomings are also made obvious. Burris remarks that Castle can be open-minded and can entertain all kinds of positions in an argument until he reaches his final decision and then closes his mind and refuses to consider any more alternatives. In this way Castle has latched on to the term "Fascist" to explain Frazier once and for all; everything Frazier does from this time on Castle interprets as an indication of Frazier's fascism. Castle's analysis of the anti-humanistic content of Walden Two is, however, quite accurate at times. In our discussion so far we have developed some of Castle's arguments.

Rogers and Barbara are the young couple who do not remain in Walden Two after the five-day visit. Rogers is portrayed as a sensitive and intelligent young man who is looking for a more rational and meaningful way to live than that afforded in port-World War II American society. Rogers is impressed by what he sees in Walden Two and would like to remain. It is, in fact, precisely what he has been searching for. His problem is that he cannot do without his pretty, blonde fiancee, Barbara Macklin. Barbara is portrayed as a somewhat limited, dense and naive girl, totally conditioned by the values of the society outside Walden Two. She is such a child of her own society that she cannot even entertain the possibility of alternatives. Since Rogers is unable to live without her, he sacrifices the hope of a personally rewarding life in Walden Two for a life of strife, competition, material affluence, and bourgeois conformity with Barbara.

Steve Jamnik and Mary Grove have nothing to lose and everything to gain by joining the Walden Two community. Unlike Rogers and Barbara, they are children of low income families from "somewhere across the tracks." Walden Two offers them a chance to escape from the dismal environment which their economic status forces upon them. Outside Walden Two, they have only limited opportunities - poor jobs, shabby housing, children playing in slums. Inside Walden Two, there is no economic discrimination and hence their possibilities for a rewarding life are immeasurably increased. They both realize the advantages that Walden Two offers and are elated when they discover that they can spend the rest of their lives in the community.

WALDEN TWO: UTOPIA OR ANTI-UTOPIA?

We are not in a better position to come to some evaluation of Walden Two as a utopia. We have already noted that even though Skinner intended his novel as a positive image of the good society, many readers have equated it with such anti-utopian patterns as Orwell's *1984* and Huxley's *Brave New World*. Some of the reasons for this are immediately apparent: Walden Two is ruled and maintained by a few technocratic managers and planners, Walden Two is concerned primarily with eliminating the experiences of doubt, uncertainty, anxiety - even to the point of making ethical behavior automatic; and most important, Walden Two requires the surrender of human freedom and autonomy.

Nevertheless, Skinner's motivations in *Walden Two* share certain features with the utopian tradition. Like other utopian thinkers, Skinner's strategy is to contrast the possibilities of life within Walden Two with life outside. In this way he is able to demonstrate his discontent with the way things are arranged in our society (a strong indictment of the present) and at the same time to show that things are not immutably fixed but that there is hope for a better man and a better world. Furthermore, Skinner shows that things will not improve by themselves but only through careful planning and through a change in our conception of man from a vague humanistic image to a rigorous scientific one.

It is because of the anti-humanistic content of Skinner's scientific utopia that it has been so furiously attacked at times. In these attacks the beneficial aspects of Walden Two are often overlooked. We would like, therefore, to summarize the positive achievements of Walden Two before making an overall judgment.

Walden Two does achieve some important utopian aims that should not be overlooked:

1) We have seen that the overall strategy of Skinner's utopia is the elimination of coercion, threat, and punishment in favor of the techniques of positive reinforcement. Walden Two is engaged in promoting the general welfare - happiness, tranquility, contentment - by eliminating aversive control from the environment.

2) The work system in Walden Two is designed to eliminate menial, debilitating labor through automation and technology. Walden Two tries to exploit the liberating potential of technology (there is no longing here for a mythical, pastoral past) not for maximum production, but rather just enough to maintain the general welfare.

3) Walden Two eliminates the negative aspects of a consumer-oriented society. There is no advertising industry that creates pseudo-needs for worthless products; there is no tasteless and chemically poisoned frozen food; no compulsion to buy and own more and more useless gadgets. There is no affluence in Walden Two, but there is also no poverty and human depravity.

4) A great deal of emphasis in Walden Two is given to the training and education of children. No matter what we may think about lollipop training, the aims are to ensure that children will be self-controlled, tolerant, cooperative, and free from resentment. Communal upbringing is designed to strengthen cooperative values and group orientation; hence Walden Two precludes the kind of individualism that results in inequities and injustices.

5) Walden Two is an egalitarian society that eliminates racial, sexual, and economic prejudices. Distribution of wealth

is equal and there is complete sexual equality. Perhaps some of the intensity and variety of experience has also been eliminated, but in utopia general well-being is a higher value than intense individual experience.

6) There is peace and security in Walden Two. Unnecessary pain and suffering have been eliminated, and aggression and the will to dominate have been suppressed. Social relationships in Walden Two are founded on tolerance and mutual affection.

Walden Two is directed toward securing the good life, and Frazier is willing to define the "good life" without getting bogged down in abstract philosophical discussion. All this, he says, is possible here and now if we maximize the potential of the experimental approach and solve the problems of social life through human engineering. Since Walden Two has apparently achieved all these traditional aims, one wonders what many readers find so objectionable? Are their objections justified?

MEASUREMENT OF WALDEN TWO'S ACHIEVEMENTS

A good way to measure the achievements of Skinner's imaginary utopia is to compare them with the potential inherent in utopian thinking and then to see whether Skinner's vision approximates these potentials or falls short. Utopian thinking is essentially an imaginative vision of human possibilities. Utopian thinkers offer an image of man and society that is optimistic and progressive, and that opens up new possibilities for the future. In their hopes for a new perspective on man and society they reflect a basic discontent with the status quo and desire a significant transformation of it. In their effort to enhance the quality of life, they project an image of man that is regenerative of the whole person - politically, socially, intellectually, morally. Utopian thinking should not get lost in pure fantasy, however, but rather build on what is really possible.

Skinner's blueprint for utopia reflects some of these criteria: there is general discontent with the status quo, and Skinner's imagination does not soar beyond the limits of what is feasible. Furthermore, Skinner is concerned with the question of projecting a new image of man. Toward the end of the novel, Burris realizes that what is required is "a new conception of man" and "a complete revision of culture." In *Walden Two*, however, this new conception must be compatible with the science of human behavior, and it is precisely here that Skinner's overall vision suffers. The science of human behavior, instead of extending man's possibilities, actually diminishes his potential. Instead of showing how man can be regenerated, it demonstrates how he can be manipulated. Instead of projecting new possibilities for man, Skinner demonstrates how man can be made to function smoothly and efficiently in a community. Skinner's vision is not imaginative enough; in fact, it comes perilously close to the ant-hill image. The ultimate concern in Walden Two seems to be efficiency. Frazier is outraged that at the present time our society functions at less than one percent efficiency. Walden Two may reflect precision and tidiness, but it does not project "a new conceptions of man" that opens up utopian possibilities for the future. In fact, the average member of Walden Two seems very close to the status quo. He is content and well-taken-care-of, but he seems less than a whole person.

THE PRICE PAID FOR WALDEN TWO

Perhaps more important is the fact that although Walden Two promises certainty, security, and efficiency, it does so at a tremendous price. The price we must be ready to pay for membership is the surrender of autonomy and submission to an ethical code that threatens to destroy conscious life. For many readers of *Walden Two,* this seems too high a price even for utopia. They feel they would lose more than they would gain even though Frazier promises a world without pain and suffering.

COMPARISON WITH DOSTOEVSKY LEGEND

All this brings *Walden Two* close to the realm of Dostoevsky's "Legend of the Grand Inquisitor," as Andrew Hacker and others have observed. A brief comparison here will indicate parallels and differences. Our aim is to point to possible shortcomings of Walden Two as utopia in the sense of the "good place."

The "Legend of the Grand Inquisitor" is a short monologue within Dostoevsky's novel *The Brothers Karamazov.* The story relates a second coming of Christ to earth during the Spanish Inquisition. This time Christ is immediately arrested and held in a dungeon. In the ensuing monologue, the Grand Inquisitor tells Christ that he should not have returned. The Church and Pope now rule in his name, and they have since learned that Christ had badly misunderstood the nature of man. Christ had originally brought man the gift of a free faith, but the Church fathers have established that man does not have the strength to bear the burden of freedom and all that freedom implies - doubt, anxiety, ambiguity, suffering, despair. Most men, the Church has discovered, would rather give up their freedom in favor of material comfort, security, and obedience. Through "miracle, mystery, authority," the Church satisfies these needs, and the few - the leaders - take upon themselves the responsibility of choosing between good and evil. The vast majority enjoy the benefits of this arrangement by living as contentedly and simply as "a flock of sheep."

Dostoevsky's legend points out several significant assumptions. The essential premise of the Grand Inquisitor is that men are weak and that they prefer happiness and security to all else. Secondly, the Grand Inquisitor is firmly convinced that his manipulation of men is done for the benefit and general welfare of the majority. His actions are motivated, he insists, by the love he feels for all men in their weakness. Thirdly, the story points out that those who rule, the elite like the Grand Inquisitor, have awesome power over other men.

Although Frazier does not rule by "miracle, mystery, authority," his basic assumption is also that men are basically weak. "The majority of people," he says, " ... want to be free of the responsibility of planning. What they ask for is merely some assurance that they will be decently provided for." This estimate of human nature, in addition to his denial of human freedom, brings Frazier uncomfortably close to the Grand Inquisitor.

Also, like the Grand Inquisitor, Frazier sees his manipulation of men as an act of benevolence (he refers to those he conditions and controls as his "children") and remains aloof from them. Although he insists that he has made others happy, he himself remains unhappy. (In Frazier's case, the unhappiness is the result of his poor conditioning; the Grand Inquisitor claims to suffer because he has taken on himself the anguish of choice and responsibility.)

Again, like the Grand Inquisitor, Frazier is aware of his awesome power over other men - in his case, the power of the techniques of behavioral engineering. Frazier talks about the total "design of personalities" and the complete "control of temperament." "Give me the specifications," he says, "and I'll give you the man." Like the Grand Inquisitor, Frazier seems eager and willing to assume the responsibility that this implies.

We can now see why so many readers of *Walden Two* are dismayed by Skinner's vision of a better society. One would expect that in utopia, the good place, there would be an effort made to develop and enhance man's strengths rather than his weaknesses. Although Frazier's intentions, like those of the Grand Inquisitor, are benevolent, we should not mistake the assumptions on which they are based. Furthermore, in spite of all assurances to the contrary, Skinner's utopia maintains a vast gap between those who control the techniques of behavioral engineering and those who are subjected to them. The manipulation involved brings *Walden Two* close to *Brave New World* and to the Grand Inquisitor's "flock of sheep," and hence too close to the beehive image of man to be a genuine utopia.

And finally we must ask whether Skinner's community in any sense expands human consciousness and nurtures full human beings. The relationship between the individual and the community is a crucial one for utopia, and surely one has the right to expect a balance between individual self-realization and the collective good. In Walden Two, however, the emphasis is on the efficiency and harmony of the group. Since utopia is a model for a better society, shouldn't it reflect a vision that is more desirable in all respects? And doesn't that imply at least a degree of autonomy for the individual? Certainly, if Walden Two is to be regarded as a genuine utopia, it should not come as close as it does to the nightmares of *Brave New World* and *1984*.

AN EXPERIMENT IN WALDEN TWO LIVING

Professor Skinner is often asked why he has never attempted actually to establish his fictional community based on the principles of positive reinforcement. His reply is that at one time he did seriously think about it, but decided, like Frazier, that his real interests are in developing and perfecting the techniques of his science. Skinner's argument is that his further researches may ultimately advance the principles of *Walden Two* more effectively. Furthermore, he insists, the task of realizing *Walden Two* requires younger people.

There have, in fact, been several attempts made by others, usually by younger people, to actualize the principles of communal living upon which the fictional Walden Two is based. A few years ago there was an attempt to set up a Walden Three in California, and a group of students at Grinnel College in Iowa attempted to combine the principles of *Walden Two* with a politically active approach.

But the most thorough and impressive undertaking to date is the Twin Oaks community in rural Virginia (near Louisa, Virginia), founded by Kathleen Kinkade and others in 1967. Fortunately, the community has recently published an account of the first five years of the experiment entitled, *A Walden Two Experiment: The First Five Years of Twin Oaks Community* (1973). Summarizing briefly the problems, failures and successes reported will provide us with concrete evidence from which to evaluate Skinner's ideas. Skinner's *Walden Two* is a ten-year-old fictional community; Twin Oaks represents five years of concrete experience and practical testing.

In 1972, the population of Twin Oaks had stabilized at about forty members (which is a long way from Skinner's community of approximately 1,000). The members appear to be hip communalists (long hair, hippie clothing, sexual freedom), but any resemblance to hippie communes is only coincidental. In fact, drugs and marijuana use are expressly prohibited to members, and even visitors are not allowed to use them. Like Walden Two, Twin Oaks is actually a highly structured community that favors technology and automation as labor-saving devices. Economically, the community is sustained by agriculture, operating a small hammock industry, and through outside employment of its members. They process meats, milk, and vegetables, and maintain large freezers for their food supply. The members learned first-hand some of the ironies in attempting to establish a utopian community, e.g., when they discovered that packaged chicken from the supermarket was less expensive than buying the feed to raise their own chickens.

WAITING LISTS FOR TWINS OAKS

Financial problems have been a difficult obstacle. Although the income from the hammock sales has improved somewhat, the community still needs to supplement income through outside employment. There have been several financial crises in the past, but the community seems to have survived them intact. Any profits that are now being made are reinvested in improving housing or in buying and maintaining farm equipment. In spite of the tremendous turnover in membership in the past five years, the population seems to have stabilized and at present there are waiting lists for people who want to join.

Twin Oaks was inspired by *Walden Two*, and Skinner's utopian patterns remains the guiding force of the community. The general approach of Twin Oaks is to first try out the proposals in *Walden Two* and then to modify them in accord with the demands of the situation. This is very much in the spirit of Skinner's experimental method.

Applying this method, Twin Oaks has successfully adapted the labor-credit system of Walden Two. Even though the system breeds a mass of paper work, and even though members of Twin

Oaks work about forty hours a week, the system guarantees a fair distribution of work. Men and women share the work equally since traditional male/female work distinctions have been overcome. Needless to say, such tasks as dishwashing and general maintenance are the least desirable tasks and hence earn greater labor credit. If a member refuses to work in Twin Oaks he is simply asked to leave. This is different from Walden Two, where Frazier claims that the situation never arises.

Twin Oaks has also adopted Skinner's system of Managers and Planners and even a Behavioral Code. Although some of the members have resented the Planners as the "power structure" (the words themselves have been troublesome because they "turn people off"), the system seems to be working effectively. In Twin Oaks the terms have become synonymous with "the person responsible." The most important function in the community is carried out by the Managers who make the day-to-day decisions. The Managers can, however, be overruled by the Board of Planners, which is elected in Twin Oaks. There is, of course, no police force, and because of the simplicity of the system and the small size of the community there is no bureaucracy. The danger of members with dictatorial ambitions seems minimal since there is nothing to be dictatorial about. The essential aim of the community is to establish a non-competitive culture, to simplify life and to do away with the consumer mentality.

INTERPERSONAL PROBLEMS

The most pressing problems, ironically enough, have to do with interpersonal relations-the solution of which is Frazier's biggest boast. In Twin Oaks, interpersonal relations remain a never-ending source of conflict and friction. Disputes and disagreements have ranged from nutrition to ideology to the kind of building material and designs to be used. The Behavioral Code provides some guidance. It states, among other things, that members are not allowed to gossip or discuss the personal affairs of other members when they are not present. Criticism sessions and group therapy have been partially successful, but there remains a great deal of malice, resentment, and jealousy. Because of the disruptive effect this has on the community, potential members are now screened and a probationary period has been instituted for new members.

Nevertheless, the problems of interpersonal relations remain formidable in Twin Oaks. Human engineering as advocated in *Walden Two* is obviously a long way from being reality in Twin Oaks. Along with the bitter quarrels and disenchantment over organization, ideology, and design of the community, the relaxed sexual standards of the community have increased the problems of jealousy, mating competition and possessive behavior. Interpersonal friction and strife indicate that Twin Oaks is not even close to the smoothly functioning society that Skinner described. Nor has Twin Oaks been able to apply consistently the principles of positive reinforcement. The community still relies a great deal on aversive measures - rules, propaganda, subtle coercion.

PROBLEMS IN CHILD-RAISING

This failure is perhaps most evident in the community's attempts to apply Skinner's views to the management of child behavior. As in *Walden Two*, the aim of the Twin Oaks community is to phase out the traditional "nuclear" family and replace it with the communal raising of children. The community even invested in a commercially sold "Aircrib" when the first child was born, but returned it (it was a "rip-off") and built their own according to

Skinner's specifications. They appointed a Manager of Child Behavior, and the entire community shared in the child-raising process. The problems that arose, even when the biological parents accepted communal child care, were enormous. Constant disputes over training, education, and control brought about a situation in which the admission of children had to be temporarily prohibited. This is a significant failure since, as we have seen, the raising of children is the most crucial activity in Walden Two.

SKINNER'S CRITIQUE OF TWIN OAKS

How does Skinner view this experiment? In the Foreword to the book Skinner confirms that Twin Oaks is not yet Walden Two. Since the scientific principles of human engineering are not consistently applied, one suspects that it may not even be a genuine experiment. The biggest hurdle, Skinner reaffirms, is the problem of personal relations brought about by aversive and punitive measures. As long as positive reinforcement cannot be consistently applied, communal utopian living remains difficult. But Skinner feels that Twin Oaks is on the way toward Walden Two. The real test, he says, will come with the raising of children. Only with a generation that is not the product of aversive control can there be any real test.

As a community, however, Twin Oaks seems to have "muddled through" to apparent success and relative stability. But it is still a long way from utopia. Financially, the community still depends a great deal on outside society, and much needs to be done to raise the standard of living. But the members feel that they are getting closer and are certain that they are going in the right direction toward the "good life." At present, they are at least able to offer an alternative, and providing an imaginable alternative, as we have seen, is the first step toward utopia.

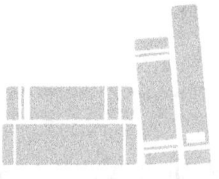

BIBLIOGRAPHY

SKINNER'S MAJOR PUBLICATIONS

The Behavior of Organisms. New York: Appleton-Century-Crofts, 1938.

Walden Two. New York: Macmillan, 1948. (Macmillan Paperback, 1962.)

Science and Human Behavior. New York: Macmillan, 1953.

Schedules of Reinforcement (with C. B. Ferster). New York: Appleton-Century-Crofts, 1957.

Verbal Behavior. New York: Appleton-Century-Crofts, 1957.

The Analysis of Behavior (a programmed text with J. G. Holland). New York: McGraw-Hill, 1961.

Cumulative Record, revised edition. New York: Appleton-Century-Crofts, 1961.

The Technology of Teaching. New York: Appleton-Century-Crofts, 1968.

Contingencies of Reinforcement: A Theoretical Analysis. New York: Appleton-Century-Crofts, 1969.

Beyond Freedom and Dignity. New York: Alfred A. Knopf, 1971.

About Behaviorism. New York: Alfred A. Knopf, 1974.

Selected Writings on Skinner, "Walden Two," And Utopias

Carpenter, Finley. *The Skinner Primer: Behind Freedom and Dignity.* New York: The Free Press, 1974. Although the author's main concern is to analyze the debate over Skinner's *Beyond Freedom and Dignity,* the book contains a good introduction to Skinner's overall views.

Chomsky, Noam. "The Case Against B. F. Skinner," *The New York Review of Books* (December 30, 1971), pp. 18-24. Highly critical of Skinner's entire science of human behavior. Chomsky's earlier review of Skinner's *Verbal Behavior* has become famous. See *Language*, 35 (1959), pp. 26-58.

Elliot, Robert C. *The Shape of Utopia: Studies in a Literary Genre.* Chicago: University of Chicago Press, 1970. A study of the **genre** of utopian literature. Contains a short interpretive study of *Walden Two.*

Evans, Richard I. *B. F. Skinner: The Man and His Ideas.* New York: E. P. Dutton, 1968. In dialogue form, Skinner talks candidly about his work and ideas and also provides a short defense of *Walden Two.* An excellent introduction to Skinner's views.

Fromm, Erich. *The Anatomy of Human Destructiveness.* Connecticut: Fawcett Publications, 1973. Fromm devotes one chapter to a critical analysis of Neobehaviorism. Fromm sees Skinner as "a naive rationalist who ignores man's passions."

Hacker, Andrew. "Dostoevsky's Disciples: Man and Sheep in Political Theory," *The Journal of Politics,* 17 (1955), pp. 590-613. The author draws interesting parallels between Dostoevsky's "Grand Inquisitor," Huxley's *Brave New World*, and Skinner's *Walden Two*.

Kateb, George. *Utopia and Its Enemies.* London: The Free Press of Glencoe, 1963. The author seeks to be defend utopian thinking against the most frequent attacks. The lengthy discussion of Skinner's utopia is eminently fair, defending *Walden Two* against some of its critics, but also indicating shortcomings of Skinner's utopia. In this admirably balanced study, Mr. Kateb points out that anti-utopianism involves dangerous anti-social tendencies.

Kinkade, Kathleen. A *Walden Two Experiment: The First Five Years of Twin Oaks Community.* New York: William Morrow & Company, 1973. One of the founders of the Twin Oaks Community depicts the struggles, failures, and successes of the first five years of an actual Walden Two experiment.

Koestler, Arthur. *The Ghost in the Machine.* Chicago: Henry Regnery Co., 1971. Contains a devastating attack on Skinner and Behaviorism. Koestler sums up Skinner's psychology as a "monumental triviality."

Krutch, Joseph Wood. *The Measure of Man.* New York: Harcourt Brace, 1954. A vigorous attack on Walden Two as an "ignoble utopia" and on the probings of Skinner's science of man. Krutch's intention is to defend human dignity against the conditioning and control he sees in Skinner's ideas.

Manuel, Frank E., ed. *Utopias and Utopian Thought.* Boston: Houghton Mifflin co., 1966. An excellent collection of essays on various aspects of utopian thought.

Roberts, Ron. *The New Communes.* Englewood Cliffs: Prentice-Hall, Inc., 1971. Thoughtful and insightful description of utopian movements now occurring in the United States.

Rogers, Carl R. and B. F. Skinner, "Some Issues Concerning the Control of Human Behavior," *Science*, 124 (1956), pp. 1057-1066. Famous debate between Skinner and Rogers (a phenomenological psychologist) at a symposium. Skinner provides a clear **exposition** of his ideas on control.

Skinner, B. F. "Visions of Utopia," *The Listener* (January 5, 1967), pp. 22-23 and "Utopia through the Control of Human Behavior," *The Listener* (January 12, 1967), pp. 55-56. Two lectures Skinner delivered at a symposium on utopias. In the first lecture Skinner provides a valuable and informative sketch of the history of utopian thinking. In the second he deals with his premise that today utopian thinking must be based on scientific control and argues against the fear that this raises in many people's minds.

www.ingramcontent.com/pod-product-compliance
Lightning Source LLC
LaVergne TN
LVHW011736060526
838200LV00051B/3185